A Childfree Happily Ever After

WHY MORE WOMEN ARE CHOOSING

NOT TO HAVE CHILDREN

TANYA WILLIAMS

First published in 2018 by Grammar Factory Pty Ltd.

© Tanya Williams 2018

The moral rights of the author have been asserted

Printed in Australia by McPherson's Printing
Cover design by Designerbility
Editing and book production by Grammar Factory

ISBN (paperback): 978-0-6481372-6-9
ISBN (eBook): 978-0-6481372-7-6

NATIONAL
LIBRARY
OF AUSTRALIA

A catalogue record for this
book is available from the
National Library of Australia

Disclaimer

The material in this publication is of the nature of general comment only, and does not represent professional advice. It is not intended to provide specific guidance for particular circumstances and it should not be relied on as the basis for any decision to take action or not take action on any matter which it covers. Readers should obtain professional advice where appropriate, before making any such decision. To the maximum extent permitted by law, the author and publisher disclaim all responsibility and liability to any person, arising directly or indirectly from any person taking or not taking action based on the information in this publication.

CONTENTS

PART TWO – MAKING THE RIGHT CHOICE FOR YOU

This book is for my fabulous husband Shayne,
who has always accepted and supported my decisions and
taken this journey with me, holding my hand
as my partner along the way.

I love you all the way round the world and back again.
I can't wait for our happily ever after. xoxo

PREFACE

I first started writing this book several years ago when I was interviewed for a national newspaper magazine about my choice not to have kids. In the interview, I freely shared my journey and choices. While I had always thought I was in a very small minority, one thing that story highlighted was that there are so many of us out there who share the choice to be childfree, whatever the reason might be.

Though I thought we were a rare breed, it seems our breed is gaining in popularity. It is refreshing to see that we are not all clones doing what we are told is right and natural for women, or 'our duty', but are making decisions based on what's right for us.

That realisation set me on the journey of writing this book about the decision not to have children – a book that explains where we've come from and why this decision is still seen as controversial in our modern world. It's also written to help other women – childfree or undecided – find the right path for them.

For me, this was an informed decision that I made when I was very young. I have never regretted it because it was made consciously and willingly. Unfortunately, the decision has also come with consequences, and a lot of judgement.

For some reason, society has a really difficult time wrapping their minds around the fact that some women simply do not want to procreate. Perhaps it is something that they have to put in a box or label as: 'I don't understand it, therefore, it is weird or wrong'.

My question is: Why is it okay to question one woman's decision not to have kids, yet, not okay to question another woman's decision to have them? Is a woman's life only valuable if she is taking care of other people?

I wouldn't choose to become a dentist on the chance I might love the career once I get there. So why should I do the same when it comes to having kids? Yes, I might like it, but I also might not. And the fact is, if you know yourself, you know what you want. Children are not like dying your hair a different colour, or choosing what to study at university. It is a responsibility you have for life, so why should any woman be forced to do something she knows isn't right for her?

Unlike a career choice or a pair of shoes, you cannot change your mind when it comes to having a child.

As a childfree woman, I am enough. I am a full-time wife, I run a full-time business, I am a full-time mum to my three fur kids, and I am full-time experiencing as much as I possibly can during the little time we have here on earth. I think you should, too.

I am not anti-kids; I am anti-kids-for-me. I'm not telling you that you shouldn't have kids, or that you should. I'm saying is that you should be free to make the right decision for you. And, whatever decision you make, I respect and support you.

I am very passionate about what I am writing about in this book. It is my life's work, so to speak. You likely won't agree with everything I have written and that is okay with me; I don't expect you to.

However, before we get started, please let me clarify that this book is not about bashing mums or women who choose to have kids – I promise! I am fully accepting and supportive of other women's choices. And throughout this book, I share stories from all perspectives; women who are childfree by choice, women who have them and are happy, women who are childless by consequence and women who regret having children. I wanted to share their voices, too.

This book is a field guide – an anthropological study of why we feel the pressure to have kids, and the different factors that influence our decision. It's intended to shed some light on why you might feel the way you do, and help you reconnect with your authentic self and what you really want.

This book is dedicated to those women like me who have decided to live a different and equally fulfilling and adventurous life *sans* kids. Those brave enough to defy tradition, peer pressure and judgement, and do what is right for them instead. Those brave enough to say: 'Fuck you! I make my own choices.'

And this book is for those who support them in the choices they have made to live the lives they want. My desire is that it changes the acceptable social narrative around being childfree.

"You cannot live your life looking at it from someone else's point of view."

PENELOPE CRUZ

INTRODUCTION

It is a fact that more women than ever before are choosing not to have children. Due in part to birth control, later marriages, the emergence of two-career couples and changing priorities, this trend is now evident worldwide.

Just consider how childlessness has grown in all OECD countries. Australia has the second highest rate of people not having children. According to the 2016 census figures, 2,935,710 women over the age of fifteen in Australia had never had a child. The corresponding figure in 2006 was 2,422,435. In 2016, about sixty-four per cent of women aged twenty-eight had no children – a stark increase from the fifty-eight per cent of twenty-eight-year-old women in 2006 who didn't have a child.

The Australian Bureau of Statistics estimates that twenty-four per cent of Australian women will never have children and predicts that the number of couple families without children is set to overtake those with children in either 2023 or 2029. Childfree-couple households will increase by 1.4 million to 3.5 million over the 2006 to 2031 period.

In Australia, Germany, Italy and the US, the proportion of childlessness among women in their late forties has doubled over the past three decades.

Our neighbouring women in New Zealand are also braving the decision to remain childfree. In 2016, approximately thirty-one per cent of New Zealand women were childfree.

In the UK, one in five British women will end their childbearing years without having a child, many by choice. In the US, forty-two per cent of the American female population is childless, representing the fastest-growing demographic group to emerge in decades. New data shows Canadian couples are having fewer children, partners with children making up 26.5 per cent of households in 2016 compared to 31.5 per cent in 2001. In a reflection of the decision that more women are making not to have children, more men and women are also opting for sterilisation at an earlier age.

According to 2017 estimates from the CIA's World Factbook, America's Total Fertility Rate is 1.87. Figures in Europe were even lower: 1.45 in Germany, 1.43 in Greece, 1.5 in Spain, and 1.44 in Italy. A Center for Disease Control and Prevention analysis found that, in 2016, America's general fertility rate, which measures the number of women aged fifteen to forty-four who have children in a given year, slipped to sixty-two births per 1,000 women, a record low since measuring began. That trend speaks volumes about the choices women are making in modern society.

Meanwhile, those who *do* choose to have children are having them much later than they did in the past. In Britain, the birth of Kate Middleton's first child highlighted this trend. Kate, at thirty-one, was over a decade older than Princess Diana was when she gave birth to Prince William. Things have changed a lot in a generation and the number of first-time UK mothers in their forties has risen by fifteen per cent in the last five years.

The online world provides further proof that the childfree phenomenon is alive and growing. No Kidding is a member group that was founded in Vancouver in 1984, with thousands of members ranging from eighteen to eighty. It is not a dating service, but a social club for adults who have chosen not to have children. There are also online groups like Childfree.net, which is a group of adults who all share the desire not to have children of their own. The group includes teachers, doctors, business owners, authors, computer experts – you name it – from all over the world and of all ages.

Yet, despite the growing trend towards childlessness, with twenty-five per cent of women born after 1975 expected not to have children, the number of women who openly admit that they don't want children hasn't changed.

Why? Because not wanting kids is seen as a social *faux pas*, with Australian women experiencing social exclusion if they choose to remain childless, particularly from other women. There is an expectation that women should have children. Children grow up being told they'll become parents one day, parents expect to become grandparents, and having children is universally endorsed as a good thing for all. As a woman, it's seen as your ability, birthright and duty to procreate.

But the truth is, times are changing. We live in a multicultural world and everyone is different. We have different religions (or even no religion), different political beliefs, different views on how children should be raised, and different beliefs about what happens when we die. While society is growing accustomed to differences of opinion in all of these areas, the subject of choosing to be childfree is a difference that is often unwelcome and makes many uncomfortable. Suddenly, everyone has an opinion! Family, friends, perfect strangers, the media, politicians and more all feel like they have a right to have a say about what is right or wrong for our personal circumstances.

This is highlighted in *Childproof*, a hilarious podcast and comedy series created by Tony Martin and Geraldine Quinn. The show is an honest and comedic take on the different lifestyles between those with kids and those without. They have the balls to explore somewhat tricky and taboo subjects in a real and damn funny way. If you haven't seen it, then I urge you to check it out. Pure genius!

On a more serious note, a recent Deakin University study led by PhD candidate Beth Turnbull has confirmed that childless women experience stigmatisation and social exclusion. 'It was really devastating reading a lot of the data,' says Turnbull. 'Some women felt that they were excluded from society and that it affected their mental health daily. They felt mothers were valued and that women with no children were not.'

So, what's the cost of the prevailing pressure to procreate?

THE COST OF ENFORCED MOTHERHOOD

I ask what purpose it serves for women to become reluctant mothers, apart from making someone else feel better.

While *not* having a child impacts only you, *having* a child impacts you, the child and their personal development, the father (or other co-parent) and even society, when you think about the person that child will grow up to become. If you decide you don't want the child after all, there are also ramifications for the taxpayer supporting that child in the system.

For many women, choosing to have kids can mean packing up their diplomas, jobs, careers, wildest fantasies, desires and goals in a box that gets stored at the back of the cupboard for the next eighteen years. Unsurprisingly, more and more younger women are considering that the obligations and responsibilities of being a mum may stop them from being able to pursue their life and career goals when it comes to their decision to have children.

Many don't want to leave behind the life that they love when they are pushed or encouraged to take the well-worn path, especially since this yellow brick road might not lead them where they expect or bring them the treasures they most desire, as the Tin Man, Lion and Scarecrow found out. And, unlike Dorothy, you cannot just click your beautiful, red-soled Louboutin's and get back to where you truly want to be.

For many women, children cost them their dreams of travel, living in other countries, starting businesses and more.

This then leads these women to feel resentment toward their partner, family or whoever pressured them into having the child in the first place, causing issues in their relationship. Other women suffer from depression, anxiety or any number of mental illnesses which can be triggered by pregnancy and birth, leading to a range of adverse effects, including an increase in suicides.

If I were forced to have a child, I know it would trigger resentment, which would then affect my relationship with myself, my husband and the child. Resentment is not a healthy way to start a relationship in any circumstances, especially not the relationship between a mother and child. Though many women try to hide this, children are very sensitive and the negative impact on a child's psyche from knowing they weren't wanted can be immense.

And what of the financial implications? Having a child is not cheap and the investment can severely impact you for the rest of your life. From an income perspective, it can also cost years in potential career growth and promotions, and lost earning potential due to the time spent away from the career ladder.

We all have an internal compass that guides the decisions we make in life and helps us make choices based on what is important to us. When society and other people get in the way, though, they act like a magnet. When you put a strong magnet near a compass, it stops working the way it's supposed to, pointing to the magnet instead of magnetic north. The same thing happens when external forces put pressure on our own intuitive compasses. When friends, family, society and the media start pressuring us to make a decision, it clouds our judgement, and our internal compass doesn't work the way it's supposed to.

This can then lead to women making a decision that's wrong for them, leading to regret and resentment.

For women who want children, the costs are worth it for the little person they bring into the world. However, for the women who aren't sure if they want children, and those who know they don't but cave to pressure from family, friends and society, a child is a very heavy burden to bear.

Forcing or strongly encouraging a woman to do something that she doesn't want to do goes against the very nature of all the things we are taught not to tolerate in modern society. So why are there different rules when it comes to a women's right to choose motherhood?

It is a choice that will massively change your life and it cannot be reversed. It is not to be taken lightly.

I, for one, do not want to look back and regret decisions I made in my life. Having a child for someone other than myself is one I would definitely regret.

We owe it to ourselves to live a happy and fulfilling life, after all. We only live once and this is not a dress rehearsal!

IT'S TIME FOR A NEW PARADIGM

After all these years of feminism and women being told they can do anything, why does our decision not to have children remain under scrutiny by psychologists, politicians, statisticians, society, the media and mothers? Womanhood equalling motherhood has long been accepted as the norm for women's lives.

Isn't feminism about giving women choices? And shouldn't those choices extend to whether or not you want to have children?

This is what we'll be exploring throughout this book.

Let's get the terminology right to start with. I am childfree, not childless, and this book is about the decision to have children or to be childfree. You are child*free* by choice and child*less* by circumstance.

With the numbers of childfree women increasing around the globe, it's time to recognise that this is a valid option, and that childfree women are reshaping the definition of womanhood in a fundamental way. Unfortunately, they are largely misunderstood, judged, criticised and scorned.

And this pressure, these expectations, can make some women feel compelled to make a decision that's wrong for them, or to put off making a decision only to change their minds later.

Regardless of your choice, this is a decision that you should be allowed to make based on what you want. Having a child, or being childfree, should never be something that you do due to obligation, tradition, expectation or because all your friends are doing it.

With this in mind, the goal of this book is to unveil some of the different forces that might have been turning you away from what you truly want, or diluting the strength of your inner voice, as well as to help you make a decision that's right for you.

No one should tell you what you can and can't do with your life. It is all about choice. And I am childfree by choice.

SO, WHO AM I TO SHARE THIS STORY?

Let's start with the facts. I'm forty-six years old. I've been happily married for twenty-three years. I believe my reproductive organs work but I don't have children and, shock horror, I don't want them. Yes, I am deliberately barren!

From a young age, I knew I didn't want children. I grew up in the seventies and eighties and, while I remember playing 'mums and dads', I don't ever remember thinking that would be the life for me. When other girls at school would talk about getting married and having kids, it didn't sound appealing to me at all. In fact, it sounded very sad to me. It sounded like a prison.

I wanted a career, to travel and to have amazing experiences. I wanted to be like the characters I read about in Jacqui Collins novels and watched on *Dallas* and *Dynasty* – rich and powerful women who lived glamorous lifestyles, got whatever they wanted and didn't need a man to make them fulfilled or happy. I wanted lifestyle, riches, career, power and the thrill of grabbing the world by the balls. (You can see the influence eighties' soaps may have had on my choices.) Nowhere in my fantasy was there room for babies, basinets and burping. And I didn't understand why you would settle for less than you wanted.

So, after graduating from high school, I started my Bachelor of Communications at the University of Newcastle with the goal of being a journalist. Unfortunately, I hated university and I was in a hurry to get out in the world and start my career and earn some money.

I started working full time at Sizzler (a job I hated) then moved into retail as a Trainee Manager at Woolworths. On what seemed like an uneventful day, I had a head-on car accident – one that should have killed me. When you see your life flash before your eyes, it makes you sit up and consider whether you are happy with the direction your life is taking. I decided it was time to make some changes, so I did a PR and marketing course and then moved into a junior marketing role to learn from the ground up.

I got my work ethic from my dad, who was a train driver and also drove trucks part time. He worked up the ranks, which often involved long hours, and I saw the value in hard work. Somewhere along the way, I also picked up the entrepreneurial bug and have launched various entrepreneurial ventures over the years.

From the beginning, I was career focused, and I never wanted to get tied down. In fact, I remember when I started dating my now husband, Shayne, I kept telling him that I didn't want to get serious. I was nineteen at the time, so that made perfect sense to me. Who thinks about long-term relationships at *nineteen*? However, it wasn't long before that all went flying out the window and I realised how special he was. There was no way I was letting him go.

When it seemed like we were getting serious, I told him that I didn't want kids, now or in the future, and if that was something that was important to him, then we didn't really have a future. I knew myself and I knew I had no intention of changing my mind. Certainly not because of something someone else wanted.

Luckily, Shayne has always been supportive of my decision. He said he could live with or without kids – it was up to me. Shayne believed it was my body and, as a female, I could choose what I wanted do with it. I find that attitude to be rare and very respectful in a man, and it's just another reason why I fell in love with him.

Shayne and I have a great life together. He is a boilermaker by trade and, luckily for me, he has been okay with us moving around the country (often with just four weeks' notice) as I've dragged him from one job to the next in my quest for adventure and to move up the corporate ladder.

In 2000, we moved from our hometown of Maitland in the Hunter Valley to Cairns in Queensland – 2,500km from home.

I never felt like I belonged in Maitland. It was full of reminders of the traditional choices being made by the people around me. Leaving school, getting a job, buying a house, getting married and having kids. And, as far as I could see, not much else. Everyone's lives were filled with domesticity and that was not a life I wanted.

While I respect their choices and I care about their happiness, sometimes I wonder if the life they have chosen is one of obligation, or if they are just ticking the boxes as they move through life. Did they honestly want to have children, or did they believe there was no other choice? What if they feel like they made a horrible mistake? There is no doubt that motherhood changes lives, but is it a change they were ready for or even wanted?

Where some people see stability, I see boring, dull and uneventful. The loss of freedom is something I cannot begin to fathom. For me, it was non-negotiable. I would not sacrifice my freedom for anyone or anything. Unsurprisingly, I always felt like an outsider there (and still do).

When I broke free, it helped me to grow as a person – to really understand who I was and what I wanted in life. I felt like an eagle that had been allowed to soar.

Today, I am well-educated, effervescent, energetic, passionate, driven, loyal and compassionate. I have always loved education. In my role as Chief of Everything in my own business, Digital Conversations, I always have to be learning, and choosing the right tactics for my clients, much like I have to choose the right tactics in life for me.

I love my life. I have a man whom I love even more now than I did when we got married twenty-three years ago. We have raised six fur babies (rest in peace Nike, Harley and Jazz), and there is nothing like coming home to Tia, Latte and Neo's wagging tails and unconditional love and affection. I have lots of great friends and surround myself with positive, happy people. I have a nice house, enjoy driving my Lexus and have many beautiful possessions (including an impressive range of Jimmy Choo's).

Shayne and I have lived all over the country and have been very lucky to design a lifestyle that allows us to travel extensively. Over the years, we have holidayed in Europe, Vanuatu, Perth, Melbourne, China, Singapore, Hong Kong, Bali and taken several trips to New York, LA and London, to name a few. One of my goals this year is to go the airport and just jump on a plane to anywhere. (Not the usual, planned-within-the-hour travel itinerary from this control freak.) I want a life filled with achievement, adventure and amazing experiences. Yep, I want it all and plan to have it all.

We have bought property, started an online shoe business, invested in shares, dined out in our favourite restaurants, spoilt our nieces and nephews and devoured many gourmet meals and bottles of our favourite beverages. We have also been able to indulge in our passions – for me, that involves buying shoes (lots of shoes), beautiful clothes and all things pink and sparkly, and indulging in long girls' lunches and the wine and champagne that goes with them. For Shayne, this involves watching football, V8 supercars and greyhounds (and, of course, spending time with me).

I am vain. I do not leave the house without at least minimum makeup and my nails and toenails are always painted. I get my hair professionally blow-dried every week and would not be caught dead outside the house in tracksuit pants, pyjamas or thongs (unless I'm at the beach, and then they are usually pink or sparkly, if not both).

I am stubborn, impatient and often expect people to keep up with me (I move at a fast pace). My favourite place to relax is beside my pool with a chick lit book. I love trash TV and I dream of being on *Real Housewives of Brisbane,* although I'd certainly be the odd one out, as I don't do Botox, fillers or any sort of plastic surgery.

I cannot cook. My dog Tia literally hides when I go near the toaster in expectation that the smoke alarm is soon to follow (I make a fabulous salad, though). I'm happiest anywhere near water, travelling with my hubby or cuddling my dogs. I like to keep fit, thrive on being busy and count down to wine time at the end of the day.

My current lifestyle is not one without responsibility. My business is a 24/7 endeavour, just like a real child. I have my three fur kids – my chosen children. I have mortgages and bills to pay.

All in all, I have a full, busy and happy life. And I would not change it for anything. I would certainly not change it for children. That does not make me a monster or a crazy person. It makes me a woman who wants to live her life by her own rules. I like living in my childfree bubble.

I believe you need to live your life for you. Not for your mother's dream or for your best friends. Live your life for you. Would you choose a career as a nurse because your mum was a nurse and her mum before her? How is it any different when it comes to carrying on the family tree? Are you chasing a dream that is someone else's?

Blaze your own trail. Your parents and friends will get over it.

PART ONE

How did we get here?

'When I was five, my fantasy was to have a **hundred dogs** and a **hundred kids.** I realised that so much of the **pressure I was feeling** was from outside sources, and I knew I wasn't ready to take that step into motherhood. Being a **biological mother** just isn't part of my experience this time around.'

KIM CATTRALL

HOW WE ARE RAISED TO BECOME MOTHERS

As an adult, it's easy to see where the pressures and expectations around having kids are coming from. It could be your parents commenting on becoming grandparents, friends asking you when you're planning to have kids (very common after getting married!) or even strangers and acquaintances assuming that you have kids, because you're of a certain age.

But where does it start?

It might surprise you that, from the day we're born, most little girls are primed to become mothers. It's in the stories we're told, the toys we play with and even the education we're given. In this chapter, I'll share an overview of some of the early influences you might not even have noticed until now.

THE LIES OF HAPPILY EVER AFTER...

We all know the story of Cinderella – a girl whose father remarries a woman with two daughters. After her father's death, her stepmother and stepsisters force her to become their servant, and she spends her day doing their chores and sleeps near the fireplace, earning the name 'Cinderella'.

When the Prince invites all of the ladies in the kingdom to the royal ball, Cinderella's stepfamily won't let her go, and she cries in despair. Her Fairy Godmother appears and transforms Cinderella from a servant into a lady with a beautiful dress, carriage, coachman and glass slippers, with a warning that she needs to return by midnight, after which the spell will be broken.

At the ball, the Prince is enchanted with Cinderella, who flees at midnight before he can learn who she is. She loses one of her glass slippers in her hurry to leave.

The Prince takes the slipper and visits all of the women in the kingdom, asking them to try the slipper. When he arrives at Cinderella's house, her stepsisters try to win him over, but the slipper doesn't fit. Cinderella then asks to try the slipper. It fits perfectly and Cinderella marries the prince and lives happily ever after.

Or how about Snow White? With the help of a huntsman, Snow White flees from her home in the castle, away from the Queen who is jealous of her budding beauty.

After wandering through the forest, she discovers a cottage that belongs to seven dwarfs. She helps herself to their food, their wine, and then falls asleep in one of their beds. When they discover her, they take pity on her and allow her to stay if she cooks and cleans for them.

Meanwhile, back in the castle, the Queen once again asks her magic mirror, 'Who is the fairest one of all?' He replies that Snow White is still alive and still more beautiful than the Queen. The Queen then tries to kill Snow White herself – in the Grimms' version of the tale, the Queen makes three separate attempts, while the Disney version focuses on the famous poison apple.

Snow White takes a bite and collapses in a deathlike state. The dwarves, assuming she is dead, put her in a glass coffin – not wanting to hide her beauty. She is then discovered by the Prince, who is able to wake her from her slumber (with a kiss in the Disney version, and by dislodging the apple from her throat in the Grimms' version).

And let us not forget the fable of Adam and Eve. God created Adam and then created Eve as a companion for him. She was designed to be a creator, nurturer and mother, and intended to bear Adam's children. Notice that Eve never had a choice as to whether she wanted a child – from the very first stories of humanity, women have been told that this is our role.

These are some of the first stories we hear as children. And most of them focus on damsels in distress and the men who rescue them so they can live happily ever after.

Take Cinderella, where marriage to the Prince is the solution to all of her problems, or Snow White, where she needs to be rescued by her own Prince. The same goes for Sleeping Beauty, and even more modern retellings with intelligent, determined heroines – such as Disney's *Beauty and the Beast* and *The Little Mermaid* – continue to make marriage the end goal.

The message of these stories is that marriage leads to happily-ever-after, and the wedding day is the ultimate event in a girl's life story. That 'happily ever after' then involves having children and the mother staying home while her handsome husband goes off on adventures.

This is what we are fed from when we are very little (and impressionable) girls. Promises of Mr Right and happily ever after are dangled in front of us and portrayed as the fantasy that every little girl dreams of – a fantasy that our mums know does not exist in the way it is presented in the book.

Fairy tales are a child's world of imagination and pleasure, but they also provide a source of inspiration and role models. And the narrative is one that positions motherhood as being the predominant or first role girls are expected to fill. For thousands of years, the stories we have told young girls teaches them that a woman's only role is to get married and have babies. What role models are we providing them that show you don't have to fulfil the role of mother in order to be successful and live happily ever after?

Most fairy tales reinforce the traditional roles that we are supposed to accept and want. It's time to challenge the status quo for the next generation and teach them to be smart, sassy, independent women who can make up their own minds.

TOYS, AS DEFINED BY YOUR GENDER

As little girls, we have dolls thrust upon us with an expectation that this is what is right and what girls want. This includes dolls like BABY born®, Pregnant Mum doll, Midge (Barbie's pregnant BFF) and Mommy To Be (launched in 1991, this doll came with a detachable pregnant belly and a baby inside. According to an advertisement, the toy 'helps your child understand the mystery of new life, while maintaining the magic and fuelling the fantasy of motherhood.').

Yet, while girls are given dolls and steered towards perceived 'feminine' interests, like makeup and hairdressing, boys tend to be given toys that involve action, construction and machinery, according to

Becky Francis, professor of education at Roehampton University. The message seems to be that boys should be making things and problem solving, and girls should be caring and nurturing.

But does it actually make a difference?

My sister Kelly and I were raised the same way. We got dolls for birthdays and Christmases and, I must admit, I did love my Barbie dolls (more recently, I bought Shoe Barbie and Entrepreneur Barbie). I played with dolls, just like my sister, and had one doll called a Chrissie Doll, which was the same size as a nine-month-old baby. I loved that doll and Mum still has it in my childhood room.

Having said that, we were children of the seventies and eighties, and we also played with toy cars and trucks in the dirt, rode bikes, and played cricket and other competitive sports. Dad built us a cubby house for one of our Christmases as well. I lost track of the amount of time we spent in that cubby. We had a huge dress-up box, a mini shop set-up, Nan's old table and chairs, and our little baby cribs and dolls had pride of place. I remember playing supermarkets and 'mums and dads'. From watching our parents, we learnt what little girls were supposed to do – fantasise about being mums with babies.

Yet, I don't recall ever thinking this would be my reality one day. I didn't feel a yearning or need to be a mum. It was just a way to spend time on weekends and during school holidays.

I do confess to enjoying another kind of playtime scenario much more. That was me playing the grown-up career woman and heading off to work. I remember I would dress up in my favourite old dress of Nan's and grab a handbag that I made sure included a wallet filled with play money. I would step into a pair of old high heels and sashay out the door to my pretend car to go to work.

So, do our toys impact our choices later in life?

Opinions differ greatly on this. UK education minister Elizabeth Truss recently warned that children's toys could affect their careers. She said gender-specific toys risked turning girls off science and maths and she urged parents to buy their daughters Lego to get them interested in engineering. Meanwhile, Becky Francis believes: 'Different types of toys give different messages about what's appropriate for boys and girls to do, and have different educational content – both elements are important and might have a bearing on schooling and career choices later.'

Research by retail group Argos found that over sixty per cent of adults working in design-led jobs, such as architects and designers, enjoyed playing with building blocks as children. Even more, sixty-six per cent of those working in maths-related roles, such as accountants and bankers, preferred puzzles.

While it may seem like a trivial issue, toys help children to learn new skills and develop intellectually, says Lisa Dinella, Associate professor at Monmouth University and Principal Investigator of the Gender Development Laboratory. Dolls and pretend kitchens are good at teachings kids cognitive sequencing of events and early language skills. Building blocks like Lego and puzzles teach spatial skills, which help set the groundwork for learning math principles down the line. 'Both genders lose out if we put kids on one track and they can't explore,' says Dinella.

However, child and family psychologist Margaret McAllister argues there are more significant influences on a child›s career choice than toys. 'It›s a rather superficial approach, and all too easy, to say encourage girls to play with cars and lorries and they are more likely to become engineers, as there is no real evidence of this. It›s also far too limiting and channelling of a child›s experience; job prospects are a long way off from early play.'

McAllister believes encouraging children to explore, question, interact with others and work together has more impact. 'Rounded people with good soft skills perform best. Plus, kids have access to toys in other settings than the home, like nurseries, so you can›t really monitor what your child plays with,' she says.

When I asked the question of both my childfree and child-friendly friends, I got varying responses. Many played with all sorts of toys and games and encourage their children to do so now. Like me, it was often a mix of dolls, cars, sports and games.

And what was the end result for my sister and I?

Today, my sister is a mum. Kelly grew up wanting to be married, to have six kids (she ended up having three) and to live happily ever after. And she is the picture of domesticity. She cooks, cleans, bakes, gardens, does crafty-type things and is a very good homemaker and mother to her kids. She was never career driven, and I don't ever recall her saying she wanted to be in any particular type of profession.

In fact, my sister is just like our mum, who makes home-cooked meals, fresh cakes, slices and biscuits (my friends had lunch box envy over all the yummy treats she would make for us). Mum's house is always immaculate, with not a speck of dust to be seen. She sews, knits and can make just about anything she puts her creative hand to. Her garden is just like the house – weed-free, green and fruitful.

I, on the other hand, am the black sheep of the family. I never wanted to get married or have kids. Marriage just sort of snuck up on me, but I always knew I didn't want children. I am not domestic in any way, shape or form. I cannot cook, clean, sew, garden or make things. I kill plants, burn toast, store wine in the fridge and cannot even sew on buttons (in fact, the last time I tried, I sewed the button to the pants I was fixing as well as the pants I was wearing!).

I am the ultimate un-domestic princess. I don't see the point of cooking a cake or a chicken from scratch when you can just buy one from Woollies. I don't enjoy cooking and I am not interested in learning how to do it. I am a big believer in focusing on what you are good at and outsourcing what you are not (which is why I love my cleaner so much #undomesticgoddess). Like having babies, I must have been hiding behind the door when they handed out certificates for domestic duties.

And I am very okay with that. I play to my strengths and would rather focus my energy on what I love doing. I would rather spend the extra time that gives me on building my business, or travel, or spending time on passion projects, like writing this book.

Despite having the same upbringing, today, Kelly and I are two very different sisters with two extremely different lives.

So, maybe it is an oversimplification to suggest that gendered toys play a role in our decisions as adults. Everyone had a favourite toy as a child, but whether it was Lego or a dollhouse, it doesn't necessarily mean you grew up to be a construction worker or house-keeper. I am not an expert on this and can only consider my own experiences. I do believe we are conditioned to want to play with dolls, however, I am unsure what real evidence there is to support how this affects the choices women make later in life.

Ultimately, though, it is something to consider in combination with all of the other influences facing girls today, including fairy tales, the media, family expectations and their education. With this in mind, some big players are making an effort to address the issue of gendered toys. In May 2016, the White House held a conference on gender stereotypes in toys and media. After feedback, Target announced in 2015 that it would get rid of signs labelling toys for boys or for girls. And a UK campaign called Let Toys Be Toys seeks to get retailers to stop categorising toys and books for one gender only.

What I suggest is that you are mindful of the fact when buying toys for your children or nieces and nephews and consider the influence that you may be having, albeit unconsciously, on their future decisions.

EDUCATING FUTURE WIVES AND MOTHERS

At school, these family norms and traditions are reinforced, with home economics, textiles, woodworking and technical skills still being offered in the curriculum.

Queen Elizabeth I, who chose personal and professional satisfaction over childbearing back in the 1500s, was the original trailblazer for being childfree. During this era, women could choose one of five vocations – marriage, motherhood, domestic service, prostitution or being a nun. (I choose none of these.)

While women were educated at home, they weren't allowed to study politics, medicine or law. It took some time for this to change and in the 1700s, it was still extremely rare for women to have vocations outside of being mothers, teachers or caregivers. It wasn't until the 1900s that women were allowed to attend university, as they were seen as the less robust sex (after all, how could our tiny brains and delicate senses handle the strain of so much learning?).

It wasn't until the twentieth century, however, that real progress began to be made, achieved as part of a broader campaign which centred on a range of women's issues. This is when we saw the first-wave of the feminist movement or 'liberal feminism', better known as suffrage for women.

The concept of a woman's role is the basis for the movie *Mona Lisa Smile* in which Julia Roberts plays Catherine Watson, a progressive art history professor who dares to challenge the thoughts and ideals of the girls she teaches. In a school that teaches tradition, elocution, poise and that your sole responsibility is to be the perfect wife and mother, she is considered to be a progressive thinker. After all, the grade that matters is the one your husband gives you!

The message throughout is loud and clear – do what is expected of you. If not, we will make life difficult, as the thought of women having choices and independence goes against the moral fibre of society.

These finishing schools disguised as colleges were very popular. In the sixties and seventies, women were encouraged to learn how to cook and sew (I was a disaster in both classes) while boys learnt woodwork and technical drawing. When you looked at classes like maths and science, they were largely filled with boys, because boys were the ones who went on to be engineers, lawyers and doctors while girls were nurses or teachers, right?

Instead, consider the movie *Hidden Figures*, which shares the story of a group of black women who worked behind the scenes at NASA in somewhat junior roles, despite being highly intelligent and better qualified than the men in the senior roles. Set in the 1960s at a time when women, not least of all black women, were considered inferior in so many ways, these women came to be the heroes of the story.

I remember my mum telling me that they had to learn sewing and cooking and you didn't have the option to learn what were considered to be more male subjects, a fact that I think many of us would find hard to comprehend or accept now. After all, we want it all and want it now!

I can't imagine anyone telling me I couldn't study engineering or software development if that was what I wanted to do. Do I have to only study 'girly' subjects?

According to Researchers Susan Mendez and Moshe Justman of the University of Melbourne's Melbourne Institute, girls outsmart boys in maths and science but are shunning the money-spinning subjects at school.

Australia's biggest study of high-school students warned that girls' reluctance to study science and maths could result in lower pay. 'We found that girls simply aren't doing the subjects required in order to launch a career in the highly paid engineering or IT industries,' says Dr Mendez.

'Girls who are good at mathematics favour biology and human development, subjects that can launch a career in allied health. These professions are generally not as well-paid as other STEM (science, technology, engineering and maths) industries.'

The study shows that twice as many boys as girls studied advanced maths, although equal number of boys and girls studied chemistry. Girls were twice as likely to choose life sciences and three times more likely to study health and human development.

Google Australia's head of computer science outreach, Sally-Ann Williams, said only yesterday that women comprised only three per cent of applications to study IT at university, 'yet, we know that seventy-five per cent of all future jobs will require STEM skills and the vast majority of them are technical skills.'

How can we encourage women to become more involved? Meg Urry, the Israel Munson Professor of Physics and Astronomy at Yale University and the first female Physics Department Chair says, 'The real question is how do we keep from pushing women out, not how do we attract them.'

Urry has an answer: 'Women and men have very similar student profiles; in fact many of the top students in the physics department are women, but the differences in numbers are largely issues of climate and culture and not class material or structure.' In other words, 'cultural conditioning' discourages women from the hard sciences, in which they otherwise have the potential to excel. Women can, and do, have passion for disciplines such as physics or chemistry, but the modern climate is unwelcoming to women and their unique skill sets. In order for women to overcome these cultural boundaries, significant changes to our current educational system and workplaces must be made.

Urry believes that adopting a climate that fuels female interest by motivating students to push forward through failures will allow more women to continue pursuing their passions for science without becoming discouraged. It is noteworthy that Yale has more women in science than most other institutions worldwide.

'It's time to teach your daughters to worry less about fitting the glass slippers and more about shattering the glass ceiling.'

– ANONYMOUS

IT'S TIME TO CHANGE THE WAY WE RAISE YOUNG GIRLS

Girls can be so much more than just mothers. We can be world leaders, mentors, great educators, doctors, scientists, entrepreneurs, law makers, ambassadors for charitable causes and everything in between. We have been voice of change in many industries.

So, why, in a world filled with choices, do we still hold up motherhood as the best possible scenario for women?

It's time to change the way we raise young girls, so they know that, while motherhood is an option for them, it's not the only one.

We can start telling them new stories. Rather than watching Disney movies like *Cinderella*, *Snow White* and *Sleeping Beauty*, it's time to watch films like *Brave*, *Moana* and *Zootopia*, all of which have kick-ass female leads who don't need a man to save them.

Or how about the modern fairy tale *Shrek*, where the sassy Princess Fiona is allowed to be her authentic self as she transforms into the less physically attractive (but equally amazing, sassy and confident) Fiona. From the way she is rescued to speaking her mind and even kicking butt in a few scenes, it goes against the common narrative of waiting for a man to rescue you in order to live happily ever after. I love the message that gives to young girls, letting them know it is okay to be authentically you and not rely on a man.

It's time to let girls learn and experiment by playing with a range of different toys that stretch all of their skills – intellectual, spatial, physical and social. Just because a child is female doesn't mean she should be restricted to the pink aisle – yes, let her have her dolls, but let her play with Lego and Meccano sets, with cars and trucks, with paints and pencils and balls and hoops.

When researching this topic, it was interesting and encouraging to see many women banning stereotypical toys like Barbie dolls and encouraging their daughters to think, create and explore. The more girls think out of the box and learn different skills when they are young, the more versatile, independent and adventurous they'll be as women.

It's time to encourage girls to pursue a range of interests, both within and outside the classroom. Just because a subject might have been seen as traditionally masculine, there is no reason why a girl can't tackle it. Just look at the women in *Hidden Figures* – a girl who loves maths or science or IT or engineering might be the one to save the day.

'I don't like [the pressure] that people put on me, on women — that you've failed yourself as a female because you haven't procreated. I don't think it's fair. You may not have a child come out of your vagina, but that doesn't mean you aren't mothering — dogs, friends, friends' children.'

JENNIFER ANISTON

ADHERING TO SOCIAL NORMS

We grow up modelling our behaviour on our mothers. We have toys that teach us about motherhood. We read and watch stories about finding our Prince Charming and having our happily ever after. And, even today, domestically focused subjects have much higher enrolments of girls than boys.

You would think that, once we grew up, we'd be able to put all of that aside and focus on what *we* want. Right?

The truth is, as we enter adulthood, we're also entering a society that places a high value on motherhood and largely expects women to marry and become mothers.

Not only are we expected to have children, but we are also expected to *want* to have children. This is dictated to us by the language used in society, by the media, by our family, and it is reinforced by religion and culture.

In fact, there is so much pressure that Sydney psychologist Talya Rabinovitz works with women in their thirties and forties who don't want children but have anxiety around their choice. 'In my opinion, there is immense pressure from society to have children. Particularly as part of a woman's perceived value rests on whether she is a mother,' she says.

'It's almost as if being a mother is something every woman should aspire to; it's described as an experience so rewarding that if you don't do it you are seen as unfortunate. While some women genuinely want to have kids, many feel pressured into making a decision that may not align with their deepest values and needs. Adding to the pressure to choose motherhood is that remaining childfree can be frowned upon, if not judged outright.'

So, how do you figure out whether children are something you really want, or whether you've gotten lost in the myths and marketing? In this chapter, I'll be outlining the expectations and pressures that exist all around us, so you can reflect on which desires and plans are genuinely yours, and which have been instilled by the world around you.

CHILDREN AND CULTURE

The culture you're raised in can have a big impact on whether or not you want to have kids, with children being an expectation in many cultures around the world.

In many Eastern cultures, having children is non-negotiable. In Japan, women are expected to have children as soon as they are married.

Religious beliefs may mean *a family chooses not to use contraceptives.* In Latin America, social norms and religious tradition mean family planning services aren't available to many communities. Affordable options for accessing contraception and healthcare for remote or rural communities are in short supply.

But when income is scarce and a family is already struggling, why do parents expand their families? This happens in many poor countries like Africa, Haiti, Guatemala, West Asia, India and Latin America.

There are many social, cultural, religious and economic reasons why parents in the developing world have large families, including high child mortality rates, education for girls, religion, the need for extra labour and lack of government benefits.

In contrast to this is China, which, since 1980, has had a one-child policy. If you have a second kid, you pay a stiff fine. The policy has produced, among other things, the first huge cohort of Chinese kids to grow up in very small families. The result is that traditionally large families lavish the child with attention and expect great things in return.

Both in Japan and Norway, parents are focused on cultivating independence. Children do things alone early, whether it's walking to school or to the movies. The frames, however, are different. In Scandinavia, there is an emphasis on a democratic relationship between parents and children. In Sweden especially, the 'rights' of a child are important. For example, a child has the 'right' to access their parents' bodies for comfort and, therefore, should be allowed into their parents' bed with them in the middle of the night. There seems to be lots of different rules, before, during and after pregnancy depending on your social, religious and cultural beliefs. There is no one size fits all.

Culture also plays a major role in the way a woman perceives and prepares to be a mother.

The Quran makes it clear that once a child is conceived, it has the right to life. All life is sacred and it is never permissible to terminate a pregnancy because one fears being unable to financially support a child (or another child). It believes that when God blesses a family with a child, it should be a cause for celebration and happiness.

The birth of a child into the Hindu community is also a cause for great celebration. In Hindu texts, the Brahma Kumaris views the female body as a physical vehicle for the immortal soul. Marrying or not, having kids or not depends more on the social constricts than on Hinduism. The extended family, especially other women, will visit the mother and baby, bringing in gifts such as new clothing and food. They will be particularly excited if the baby is male. The new mother will be expected to rest for forty days after the birth, and her female relatives may want to care for the child even while it is still in hospital. Children are traditionally thought of as a sign of the family being blessed by the gods.

In Chinese culture, the woman is expected to try to be quiet during labour, as crying out will attract evil spirits to the new child. (A rule that was most certainly invented by a man.)

By and large, having a child is considered to be very positive, which can make it hard for many to understand why some people might choose to be childfree.

Cate Prince, a thirty-two-year-old Aussie in Singapore, says there are big cultural differences around the childbirth discussion. 'Many Singaporeans don't understand that I have a choice to have a baby and that I have chosen not to do so. In their culture, they live with their families after getting married and often don't move into their own homes until their mid-thirties. For them it is an expectation based on tradition.' With seventy-five per cent of Singapore being populated by people of Chinese descent, it is no surprise that this attitude exists.

Even in Australia, having children is often considered to be the natural progression after marriage. I have been asked many times, 'Why did you get married if you don't want kids?' I was shocked that someone would ask this – that someone would assume that the only reason to get married is to have children. (If that *is* the case, I didn't get the memo.) For some reason, getting married because you love your future spouse and want to be with them for the rest of your life doesn't stack up.

I think it is safe to say that Western culture is 'pro-natalist', meaning that it advocates or supports a high birth rate. The belief that everyone should reproduce and have babies as often as possible is an example of a pro-natalist approach. And, in our society, people are conditioned to ask 'when' rather than 'if' you will be having a baby.

Once you leave university or school, meet a nice guy, date for a while, get engaged and married, the next step is having a child, right? That is what society says is done, what is expected and what is accepted.

In the early noughties, then Treasurer Peter Costello was so concerned about the decline in national fertility he even urged families to have at least three children, as he spruiked the introduction of the baby bonus. 'I encourage people who can, if you have the opportunity, if you're young enough, to have one for mum, one for dad and one for the country,' Costello said in an interview with Channel Nine's Laurie Oakes.

Beyond simply encouraging women to have more children, though, there is active criticism of those who choose not to. I was shocked and appalled when Bill Heffernan announced that Julia Gillard was unfit for leadership because she was 'deliberately barren'.

And what of female politicians being subject to discrimination, sexist behaviour and judgement from their male counterparts? New Zealand Labour leader Jacinda Ardern was asked if she might end up taking maternity leave in office, just seven hours after she got her job. She stated, 'It is unacceptable that women face questions in the workplace over their motherhood plans.'

I find attitudes like these particularly insulting coming from men, not to mention maddeningly outdated and offensive. Why do male politicians think they are entitled to an opinion or to create policies about something they know nothing about? What's next? A vasectomy bonus? That kind of ignorance and uneducated opinion does not belong in parliament, let alone society.

It's not just politics, however, where double standards are rife. If you are at a BBQ, people will regularly ask women if (or when) they want children, but when was the last time you heard someone ask a man that same question?

More importantly, though, what are the consequences of these attitudes?

In Japan, the pressure to have children right after marriage has sparked a trend for Japanese woman to marry later. Some of the reasons for the flight from marriage in Japan are the same as in other rich countries. Women are better educated, pursue careers, can support themselves financially and don't see the traditional family as the only way to lead a fulfilling life.

And for those who don't want children but fall pregnant accidentally, in many cultures, they are forced to have the child anyway. In Hindu culture, for example, if a woman wants an abortion, it is only acceptable if her life is at risk.

Muslim views are shaped by the *Hadith* as well as by the opinions of legal and religious scholars and commentators. In Islam, access to abortion varies greatly between different *Muslim-majority countries*. In countries like Turkey and Tunisia, abortions are unconditionally legal on request. On the other hand, in countries like Iraq and Egypt, abortion is only legal if the mother's life is threatened by continuing the pregnancy. There is no Muslim-majority country that completely bans abortion.

Ultimately, many cultures leave women feeling like they have no choice but to have children.

MOTHERHOOD IN THE MEDIA

I grew up with strong female role models on TV. With shows like *Ally McBeal, Melrose Place, Dynasty, Dallas* and *Murphy Brown* and trail blazers like Mary Tyler Moore and Lucille Ball in the sixties and seventies. Not to mention *Buffy, Wonder Woman* and *Xena Warrior Princess*. Women who could kick some serious butt. (No wonder I turned out like I did!)

I wanted to be Amanda Woodward, the kickass power woman running her own advertising agency in *Melrose Place*. Or Alexis Carrington for those shoulder pads alone. How much influence did these power women of the eighties and nineties have on the roles of modern women?

The eighties were a time of money, decadence, stature, egos, big shoulder pads and even bigger hair. It was a time when women were declaring their independence and daring to defy the gender roles defined by society. The eighties were termed the 'me' generation, as this generation seemed only concerned about themselves and making money.

Entertainment in the eighties showed the interest society placed in financial success. TV characters lived in fancy homes, wore designer clothes and drove expensive cars. Movies like *Wall Street* and *The Secret of My Success* romanticised this type of life. The eighties became about indulgence – money, sex and drugs – and this influenced pop culture and the choices we made. The eighties defied previous rules and perhaps laid the foundation for my thinking here and now.

Yet, despite the eighties power narrative, now that these women are in their thirties and forties, the pressure to procreate is still strong. While movies like *What to Expect When You're Expecting* and *Baby Mama, Baby Boom* and *Knocked Up* show women questioning their need or want for children, these movies all share the belief that, no matter how you feel now, you will just fall in love with being a mum once the baby is born. This is simply not true for all women. Hollywood keeps perpetuating the 'being a mum is the best job a woman can have' fantasy.

And Hollywood isn't alone in this promotion of motherhood. I recently stumbled across a YouTube video by Jordan Peterson entitled 'Women at 30'. In this video, he states that 'it is a noble and heroic endeavour to have children and you should sacrifice yourself to that goal.' (If you have read this far, you will understand why I find this attitude archaic and offensive.)

Motherhood may be a fantasy, but it's a fantasy that not every woman shares. Certainly not this woman. I am with Samantha Jones from *Sex and the City* on this one – baby *not* on board!

As Diana of Sydney says, 'Societal pressures are probably the most extreme today with all of the social mediums available. It's unlikely you could ever walk past a newsstand without seeing a women's magazine asking if your eggs are getting old, which celebrity is sporting a baby bump or an article with the latest and greatest mummy bloggers and mumpreneuers. Motherhood seems to have become an all-consuming role dominating women's thoughts and conversations.'

And *because* the media perpetuates this fantasy, women who don't want to have children are considered to be abnormal, and their other interests are seen as dangerous, melancholy or degrading.

In fact, in the trailer for the documentary *My So-Called Selfish Life,* which discusses the growing number of women who choose not to have kids, one of the opening shots shows a series of US TV talk shows discussing the subject, with the mainly male panels agreeing that women are selfish. One male journalist even said, 'Have you ever seen anything more selfish, decadent and stupid?'

Similarly, in a 2013 article, journalist Kate Spicer wrote, 'Any woman who says she's happy to be childless is a liar or a fool.'

When Holly Brockwell, editor of the UK women's technology and lifestyle site Gadgette, wrote for the BBC about her decision to *get sterilized and not have children,* reaction started pouring in just a half hour after the article posted. 'The emails alone have got to be in the hundreds,' Brockwell told *Fortune* – and that was only three days after the piece went live. 'Tweets, it has to be thousands. It's been non-stop.'

Many were positive, but the negative ones more than made up for the kudos. 'The nasty ones are, "You're the worst person in the world, I hate you," and they stick with you,' Brockwell said. Some, like the man who found her phone number and insisted he could talk her into wanting kids, were downright creepy. It got so bad that she deactivated her Twitter account.

This is the sort of behaviour and judgement that needs to stop. Why is it that a choice someone else makes for their own life can make a total stranger so angry? How does it impact them and why do they object so harshly? It is something I have been trying to make sense of while writing this book.

BRIBERY TO BREED

What's even more damaging than cultural beliefs and how motherhood is portrayed in the media is the effect this has on expectations and behaviour, some of which can become so ingrained that it easily gets missed.

Anne Summers, author of the 1975 book *Damned Whores* **and** *God's Police,* writes, 'We have not disavowed that motherhood is still the central, preferable and most admired option for women. We might not overtly punish women who are not mothers, but we have our ways of letting them know they have fallen short of the ideal.'

And one of the most insidious forms of preferential treatment is financial incentives for parents.

Almost half of the world faces the same demographic problem: not enough babies are being born to keep up with an aging population. As a result, countries all over the world have been trying all kinds of measures to get their citizens in the mood for procreating. Japan is spending about $29.3 million on matchmaking events and robot babies that might inspire couples to want one of their own.

Finland gives away a maternity package of various warm-weather clothes, pyjamas and books to families of newborns – or a cash grant of €140.

In 2015, Singapore announced that every baby born would get a small bag of gifts that could include a baby sling, sippy cup and a diaper bag, among other things. Parents also receive a 'baby bonus' of about $4,400 for their first two children and $5,900 for their third and fourth. Saucy add campaigns in Singapore and Denmark remind couples that they have a civic duty inside as well as outside of the bedroom.

In 2007, Russian authorities made September 12 the country's National Day of Conception and offered women who gave birth nine months later, around the country's National Day, a chance to win SUVs, refrigerators or cash.

And in Australia, there is the baby bonus, which was introduced in the 2002 budget as a $3,000 payment for new children and peaked at $5,000.

The most traditional means of encouraging birth rates is through 'baby bounty' stipends, tax breaks, and other financial incentives for families with newborn children, which have been used in most countries facing an aging population. In France, a combination of stipends, expanded childcare options and other policy measures have been credited with increasing the country's birth rate to one of Europe's highest. Families with three or more children receive discounts across France on things ranging from train fares to movie tickets.

With a fertility rate of 1.43 – well below the European average of 1.58 – Italy has taken a controversial approach to encourage citizens to have more kids. As Bloomberg reports, the country has been running a series of ads reminding Italians that time might be running out and that kids don't just come from nowhere. 'Beauty knows no age, fertility does,' one ad says. 'Get going! Don't wait for the stork,' another says.

With a fertility rate of just 1.18 children per woman, Hong Kong faces the same challenge as many industrialised countries: Without enough young people to replace aging citizens, the populations is dwindling and economic growth is slowing. In 2013, the country proposed giving cash handouts to couples to encourage them to have kids.

Beyond outright payments, however, parents also get preferential treatment from their employers. Just think of how understanding your boss is when a mum needs to take time off to stay with a sick child.

I remember when I was working at a media company with another account manager who had a toddler in day care. I lost count of the number of times she had to leave early for one reason or another, the number of times she couldn't entertain clients and the number of meetings she missed due to child-related issues.

While I understand that kids get sick or hurt and need to be taken care of, those of us who don't have kids still have important parts of our lives, and employers are rarely as understanding towards us.

I consider my fur kids to be my children. They have four legs instead of two, but they love me all the same (even when they don't get their own way). At this same role, I was asked by my boss to attend an offsite conference which I refused to attend because one of my dogs, Nike, was really sick and I did not want to leave him. I was told that it was 'only a dog' and my husband would be home to take care of him. I doubt that my boss would've said the same thing to my co-worker about her toddler!

In another role, I was away in Sydney at a conference when my dog, Harley, fell critically ill. Harley had suffered from pulmonary hypertension and a heart murmur for several years and was on some very expensive drugs to help treat his condition. While I was away, I received a call from my husband to say Harley wasn't well and they had admitted him into hospital. His condition worsened throughout the day, until I booked a seat on the next flight so I could say goodbye to my beautiful boy before he passed away.

When I called work the next day to say I was taking a couple of days off, the regional manager tried to give me a hard time about it, saying, 'It was just a dog.' I *guarantee* he would not have said the same thing to a woman who had just lost her child. I am positive the conversation and the actions would've been totally different to what I received.

If mums can have additional time off and exceed their quota of sick days, why shouldn't the rest of us get some additional time for things that are important to us? As a fur parent, I cannot claim time off to take my fur babies to a vet or to stay at home with them when they are sick because they aren't legally classed as immediate family. Yet, most people don't think to question the system.

This is then compounded by the fact that those of us who choose not to have children are the ones funding these benefits for parents. It's adults without children who need to shoulder more than their share of the cost of family-friendly work places.

When it comes to work-life balance, 'life' is usually synonymous with personal time related to parenting. Read many of the articles and blogs around work-life balance and they reinforce this notion that life actually equals parenting. Workplace culture regards caring for your children as the most valued personal time outside work. Typically, what non-parents do with their personal time is viewed as not as 'important' as parent time. There's also the common assumption that with no kids, people must have a lot of free personal time, and that work-life balance does not really apply to them.

These two perceptions create common workplace expectations that non-parent employees can and will pick up the slack for their parent colleagues when asked, often causing resentment when the boss starts to expect the sacrifice of our personal time.

I'm not saying that parents *shouldn't* be able to take time off to care for their kids, however, why can't I have the same rights? At the risk of being shot down in flames, I'd also like to pose the question of maternity and paternity leave. If I chose to have three children, that would equate to months of paid leave. So why can't I have months of paid leave to work on a project, travel or spend time training my dogs? What's the difference? We talk so much about equality in society, yet, we are far from having it. Shouldn't every person get the same treatment, despite colour, race, sex, sexual preferences, or whether or not they have kids?

Some companies are already shifting their thinking from traditional vacation and sick leave policies to offering full-time employees a set number of days per year that they can use however they like. This reflects consistent treatment of all employees. Cali Williams Yost, who has advised the United Nations, Microsoft and Johnson & Johnson on flexible work strategies, says flex-time policies should not require asking what the employee is taking the time for; 'Instead, employees should focus on: How am I going to get my job done?' If more companies continue to create policies that treat all employees equally regardless of their parental status, it will reflect a growing acceptance of those without children in the workplace.

This is the next era for feminism: Equality for childless women. As half the adult population fifty years ago, women fought for social, economic and political equality to men. And today, at nearly half the population of women, childless women deserve the political, social and economic equality that mothers have. Flexi-time for working mums means flexi-time for working non-mums to take care of the important things in their lives, like aging parents or sick pets.

Then there is also the assumption held by many employers that they need to take into consideration time away from the office when hiring a woman, assuming that all women will decide to have children at some point. (Not considering that one in four of us no longer want that.)

Finally, there are the costs of actually getting pregnant, which don't just fall on the couple trying to conceive, but on the taxpayer as well.

A staggering one in six couples in Australia and New Zealand suffer from infertility. And while the chance of having a baby following IVF is steadily improving, the cost to the Australian taxpayer has been thrown into question. According to a new UNSW report about fertility, of the 73,598 women of all ages who started IVF cycles in 2014, one in five of them delivered a live baby.

Michael Chapman, president of the Fertility Society of Australia, stated the cost of a baby for a woman over forty equals around $100,000 compared with about $28,000 for babies born to women aged thirty. That figure almost doubles for women over the age of forty-five to around $200,000 of taxpayers' money per baby.

I am all for women making choices that are right for them, but I don't think I should have to pay for those choices. Where is the equality in that?

Taking a step back, a big question is whether the financial incentives work. Do they encourage more people to have children?

In Australia, which introduced the baby bonus scheme in 1912 and then again in the early 2000s, it was widely blamed for creating a teen motherhood problem, prompting changes in how it was paid out from 2009. Despite these issues, Australia's birth rate has remained stable at between twelve and thirteen births per 1,000 since 2000.

In Singapore, the government has done much over the years to try to increase birth rates. The evolving Marriage and Parenthood Package, introduced in 2001, is arguably one of the most comprehensive and generous in the world. There are increased benefits for working parents, including additional maternity leave provisions, the introduction of paternity leave and childcare leave, and a reduction in foreign domestic worker levies and childcare subsidies. In recent years, many employers have also become more supportive of working parents, providing nursing rooms, flexible hours and other flexible working arrangements.

Yet, Singapore's birth rate has remained below ten births per 1,000 for more than a decade. This is among the lowest in the world, sitting well below most other developed and highly educated nations.

I hope some governments are reading this and that all governments come to understand that you cannot bribe women to have children.

HOW TIMES ARE CHANGING

The good news is that our culture is changing. The world in which we live now is very different to the era of my parents or grandparents.

Lonnie Aarssen and Stephanie Altman, researchers at Queen's University in Ontario, say that in past generations, having children wasn't a choice for most women. The lack of widespread, reliable birth control plus the intense pressure to start a family left the woman's prerogative moot (or muted). These factors, the researchers' thinking goes, were major reasons the majority of women in the mid- and late-nineteenth century had children – including those who wouldn't have otherwise.

Think about how many children your grandmother had and you can clearly see the differences. My mum was one of seven children and there were many women who had a large number of children, most likely for the reasons above, rather than wanting to have so many children that they could often not support them financially.

Aarssen and Altman speculate that some of these women who didn't want children then bequeathed a reluctance to procreate to their kids, who 'inherited genes from female ancestors who were not attracted to a life goal that involved motherhood, but were nevertheless forced to endure it.' These daughters, who are now adults, 'can now freely realise the lifestyle and life course goals that their maternal ancestors wished for, but were denied because of patriarchal subjugation.'

The result is that the average number of children that a woman had in 1961 was 3.5, compared to just 1.9 in 2012.

Choosing to be childfree is becoming more and more common, and there are an increasing number of female voices across the globe that are addressing the issues of this decision, including Laura Carroll, Nina Steele, Karen Malone and Amy Blackston, all of whom are considered to be pioneers in this movement.

Laura Carroll is an editor and non-fiction writer known for her many books on the subject of children. She believes that the childfree choice is still not totally accepted as an equally valid choice as the choice to have children. 'The reason boils down to pro-natalist social and cultural messaging that has exalted the role of parenthood for generations. When we question pro-natalist beliefs and see them for what they are – beliefs – we will also see that choosing not to reproduce is just as normal as the choice to reproduce.'

Meanwhile, award-winning director Maxine Trump (no relation to the idiot in the US) is close to wrapping the film *To Kid or Not to Kid,* which aims to dispel the myth that making the decision to live childfree is weird, selfish or somehow wrong. *To Kid or Not to Kid* started when I was making the decision to not have children and I felt society was beating me up for even considering the idea. It felt like I was "coming out," and all I was doing was deciding that I didn't want kids! I had to retaliate. I grabbed my camera and started filming.'

My So-Called Selfish Life will give voice to the growing numbers of women and men who have chosen not to have kids. It's also an examination of why that choice comes with a hefty dose of judgement and stigma, why our society makes motherhood feel so mandatory, who profits from it, and what we can do to change the conversation.

Filmmaker Therese Shechter states, 'I've known since high school that I didn't want kids, so it's something I've been thinking about and discussing privately with my friends for a long time. Over the past several years, stories about not wanting children have kind of exploded out of the closet, along with the expected backlash. What my film brings to the conversation is a look at what's behind the pervasive political, historical, religious and pop culture messages that got us here in the first place.

'There's a reason people feel they have to have kids, and a reason people who go against the mainstream get punished for it. The film will connect the dots between the forces that push a message of maternal inevitability that's so ingrained we don't even notice it.

'We'll be asking the questions we're not supposed to ask about motherhood: Is having children really a woman's most important – and perhaps only – role? Is the desire to have children innate? Can we create female identities that are independent from motherhood?'

Childfree women everywhere are joining in the debate. Type '#child-free' into Twitter and you could be forgiven for thinking that some sort of revolution is about to take place. Meanwhile, there are many

Facebook groups dedicated to this controversial conversation: *The Childfree Choice, Childfree Chicks International,* hundreds of *Childfree by Choice* pages, *Happily Married Childfree by Choice, Childfree over 40s – no kids, no regrets, Childfree Chicks Confidential* and the list goes on. Social media, as well as blogs and forums – such as the site *We're (not) having a baby,* the forum *Childfree Living* and Tumblr's childfree section – are buzzing with discussions about what it's like to live without children in a family-centric society. We even have our own day, with International Childfree Day being celebrated on August the first.

Even in Hollywood, childfree characters are becoming more prominent. *Sex and the City* explored this conversation in many episodes as well as the second movie. The common theme that they supported was that motherhood was not right for every woman and they showed what it looked like from all angles: the woman who vehemently knew she did not want kids (Sam), the woman who yearned for it (Charlotte), the woman who wasn't sure (Carrie) and the woman who changed from a no to a yes due to circumstance (Miranda).

While I believe there's still a long way to go, there are encouraging signs that choosing to be childfree will one day be seen as just as 'normal' a choice as choosing to have children.

'It was not my destiny, I kept thinking it would be, waiting for it to happen, but it never did, and I didn't care what people thought... It was only boring old men [who would ask me]. And whenever they went, "What? No children? Well, you'd better get on with it, old girl," I'd say "No! F*** off!"'

DAME HELEN MIRREN

WELCOME TO THE PRESSURE COOKER

As part of my research (and as an excuse to take a break from writing with a wine in hand), I watched a movie called *The Women*. *The Women* is a movie about four friends, all with very different lives.

If you cannot figure it out from what you have read about me, I clearly identify with Annette Benings's character Silvia, the career women with the new Lexus and cute dog who is often disgusted by her friend Edie's antics as a mother of four with another on the way.

In one conversation, Silvia says, 'I'm so glad I never had children. You know, that's the last impermissible thing you can say at a party – that you don't want children.'

This comment is often greeted with stunned silence, gasps of shock or women trying to convince you that you are wrong.

The assumption that girls will grow into women, get married and have babies is all around us. It's in the books we read and the films we see. It's in the expectations of our culture, and it's even encouraged by our modern political regime. We are conditioned from the moment we are born to have children. It's our biological destiny, isn't it?

However, sometimes the greatest pressure is much closer to home – the expectations of family and friends, the judgement of those around you, and the criticism from other women.

THE SUBTLE PRESSURE OF EXPECTATIONS...

As women, one of the biggest pressures to have children often comes from your parents or family. I have friends and co-workers who have shared stories with me of not really wanting kids or sitting on the fence about kids, yet, still deciding to have them because it was what their family expected. They felt they *should* do it, because their partner or parents wanted them to have children.

Sometimes, the expectations are clear. It's the relative at a BBQ asking you when you're planning to have kids. It's your mother moaning about when you're going to make her a grandmother. It's a sibling asking if their child will soon have some cousins to play with.

And if, like me, you cringe, silently scream and pleasantly say that you're not having kids, then comes the smug, knowing, 'You'll regret it if you don't,' or 'You'll change your mind later.'

All childfree women have heard the phrase 'You'll regret it when you're older' hundreds of times. Although there isn't much research on this topic, a Norwegian Study of 5,500 people between the ages of forty and eighty found no evidence that childless adults have reduced wellbeing compared to people with children. Meanwhile, US studies show that childlessness does not increase loneliness and depression. *So, why would we regret our choice?*

Then there's 'You'll change your mind later.' I have lost count of how many times I've heard this, rolled my eyes and dismissed it. 'You'll change your mind when you're thirty.' 'You'll change your mind when your friends are all having kids.' 'You'll change your mind when you're forty.' Well, guess what? I turned thirty. My friends had kids. And now that I'm at an age that starts with a four, I'm no closer to changing my mind. Why should I? I know myself and I know who I am. I knew from a fairly young age that I didn't want children and have never deviated from that decision. My GPS is firmly set on its destination – to remain childfree.

Nikki Ingram says both of her parents are okay with her decision not to have children. However, other family members are not so understanding. 'My step-mother used to pressure me often! All she ever wanted was to be a grandmother. Her own children (she has four) all lived overseas, whereas I lived here in Australia. So, before they started having children, she was at me quite often to even just "get knocked up." She would say it tongue-in-cheek, but I know she would have been stoked if I did. Thankfully, all of her own children have now had kids, so she has her much-wanted grandchildren and leaves me alone.

'My husband's father has occasionally given us a hard time about it. After he's had a few drinks in him, he might start to feel a bit bolshy and say how he thought we would change our minds and he's so devastated that we haven't given him any grandchildren. It intrigues me that the main comment he makes in relation to our decision is, "Who's going to look after you when you get older?" I think that says a lot about him, and what his expectations are of us as *he* gets older.'

For Diana of Sydney, the pressure escalated as she entered her mid-thirties. 'Parents start talking about when you might make them a grandparent and every time you attend a social gathering with friends or family, you are eyed up and down to see if you are drinking alcohol or eating raw seafood or soft cheeses so people can get the early scoop on a possible pregnancy. I found I even had questions from friends' *children* asking why we didn't have kids.'

Forty-six-year-old Kelda Rheinberger of Sydney felt the pressure in her first marriage, when the question seemed to be *when* was she planning to have kids, not *if* she was. 'I felt the pressure for not conforming to the traditional getting married and having children. It makes you feel that you are somehow not normal and people judge you as if there is something wrong with you or your marriage for not having children.'

Having said this, other times, the expectations of our friends and family are expressed in ways that are very subtle. Your parents and other relatives might ask overtly about when you're planning to have kids, but the expectation exerts itself in other ways.

In my case, when I asked my mum what she honestly thought when I told her I didn't want children, she said, 'It was your life and your choice. It was not up to me to say what you should or shouldn't do. We were never disappointed that you didn't want children. We accepted your decision as it was your life to live as you wanted to.'

However, even though my family *say* they support my decision, there are a number of ways in which it isn't supported.

From a financial perspective, my sister has received support from my parents, including trust funds for each of her children, while Shayne and I haven't received anything. I remember having a conversation with my dad where he commented that Shayne and I didn't need any help because I had my business, so 'must be raking it in'. In reality, nothing could've been further from the truth.

Or how about gifts? When your sibling has three kids, each of those kids gets birthday and Christmas presents, not to mention the special outings with Ma and Pa throughout the year. As many people with kids know, this can add up over the course of a year. The same goes for baby shower gifts, birth gifts and birthday and Christmas presents for nieces, nephews and friends' children. Sadly, it's rarely reciprocated for my fur kids. The gesture and acknowledgement of my chosen children would make a big difference. Actions speak louder than words.

On another visit, I remember sitting in the lounge room and looking around the walls at all the photos of my sister's family – there were about fifteen photos of her, her husband and their kids, and only two old photos of Shayne and I, even though I regularly sent my parents photos of us and their fur-grandchildren. I remember thinking, 'We don't figure into their life at all, certainly not the same way as my sister does.' (Which was followed by a distraught call to my poor husband late in the night.)

I know they didn't mean to make me feel like that. I know they didn't do it out of malice, and probably weren't even conscious of treating my sister and I differently, but it still hurts. My sister also believes I haven't been treated any differently or, if I have, that it is because of our decision to move away. But my experience is very different to their perception.

This is repeated with my husband's family. They say they are fine with our decision not to have children but when it comes to actually showing us that our life choice is accepted, the same applies and it hurts.

Tracey Neagle has had similar experiences. 'My parents are very traditional. I feel there is a major gap in my relationship with my parents as I didn't have children. They have six grandchildren and three step-grandchildren so when I roll up to family events, I often feel like it doesn't matter where I am or where I sleep as it's only me (and my husband sometimes).'

For Cate Prince, being successful and independent has meant she has been treated differently to her sister who has five kids, although her parents would not likely agree. 'My sister had her first child when I was still living within the family unit and most decisions were centred around my sister and her child. She has always received financial assistance, however, I was seen as capable and financially stable, so the help always went to her. One view my sister shared with me is that because we were financially well off and successful, it was my duty to help support people like her who had five children.'

Cate's sister's comments totally floored me. Why did she have to pay a price for her success and her choices, just because her sister chose differently?

When I asked Cate if she had experienced peer pressure, her response was: 'Yes and no, this really depends on the person's social circle. I'm ten years younger than my partner so while I didn't receive pressure from my immediate friendship circle, we would receive it from his work circle. Often, we would end up at a work function where all the men are his colleagues and they bring their wives to dinner or some kind of charity event. The ladies would ask me why we weren't married (at the time) and why I wasn't having children. Wasn't I afraid of being lonely and who would look after me when I age?'

While it isn't intentional, families and friends do treat you differently when you choose to be childfree. And I can even see why that might contribute to some women having kids, even if it isn't the right decision for them.

I don't believe that is the right reason to bring a child into this world. It is the biggest commitment and responsibility you can make in life and you must want it with all your heart.

Real friends and people who love you will fully support your decisions and life choices. I have always been happy for and supported my friends when they have told me of their decision to have a child. Granted, it is not a choice I make for myself, but for me, as long as they are happy, that is what matters most. Similarly, whether they agree or disagree with my decisions, they should just care about my happiness.

THE JUDGEMENT OF THE CHILDFREE

Beyond the more subtle pressure and expectations that come from friends, family and acquaintances, some people are just outright judgy.

I remember an episode of *Sex and the City* titled 'The Right to Shoes'. Carrie attends a baby shower and is asked to take off her brand-new Manolo's because the host doesn't want dirt being tracked in. When Carrie leaves, she discovers that someone has stolen her shoes!

But when Carrie confronts her friend about the situation, the mum of three shames her for her choices, saying that spending $485 on a pair of shoes is irresponsible.

Carrie realises that, over the years, she's bought wedding present after wedding present and baby present after baby present, yet, because she isn't married and hasn't had kids, she's never had the occasion to register for gifts. Carrie then announces that she's marrying herself and registers at Manolo Blahnik, with the shoes being the one item on her registry. Love her brilliance!

While I know that *Sex and the City* is just a TV show, the experience rings true. While child*less* women (those who are unable to have kids) are offered empathy, pity and support, child*free* women (those who choose not to have kids) face judgement and criticism. There are rude questions, dire warnings about a barren future, and underlying hisses of disbelief. Yes, childless women sometimes find themselves tormented by invasive, agonising questions, but the childfree can end up being ruthlessly interrogated about the 'strange', 'unnatural' or 'selfish' decision they've made. Too often, it's all a preamble to what the interrogators really want to do, which is tell you what they did and how much better it is than what you did, in effect, launching a full-out defence of their own life choices.

As Silvia says, 'the last impermissible thing you can say at a dinner party is that you don't want kids.' This statement is often greeted with stunned silence, gasps of shock or people trying to convince you that you are wrong.

Now that I am in my forties, I think many women believe I couldn't have kids. It is not common to make this choice, so I think it makes some women more comfortable to think that I couldn't rather than know I made a choice not to. When they do find out it's my choice, that's when the judgement starts.

You know what it's like when you first meet someone and they ask you all the standard questions. I see the look I get when my response to the 'have you got kids?' question is 'oh, god, no thanks'. They are often shocked by the passion in my response.

I've spoken to many women who've had similar experiences.

After being featured in an article about the choice to not have children in 2011, Cate was approached by a man to talk about her choices before they were to be on a panel together. Cate felt the man, who was very religious and a total stranger, only wanted to meet with her to preach to her about her wrong decision and try and change her mind. 'He told me that I would never experience unconditional love, I would die alone, and I was being selfish. The selfish comment was in total contradiction to his previous statement about needing to have kids so someone would look after me when I was old. Isn't that the selfish part?'

Leah Ong has found that most judgement comes from acquaintances and strangers. 'I like to think our friends and family don't judge or criticise us; it's more people who don't know us well who find it hard to believe that we wouldn't want to have children. I have had some very nasty people say that we are not contributing to society or we must be heartless people. I respond by asking them when they last had sex – they promptly say, "That is very personal," and then get offended when I reply, "So is asking me about having children!"'

Tracey, at age forty-seven, says she has faced a lot of judgement from other women about her choice. 'I have sat at my partner's corporate events where the other wives would continually ignore me over dinner. I have been gossiped about, and I have been judged harshly because: "Well, you don't have kids!"'

Lyn Griffith has also suffered from some crazy judgements. 'I remember some dear old friends of ours telling us we were quality people and therefore robbing the gene pool of good children by not procreating.'

Similarly, Nikki Ingram says, 'I do get the occasional judgement from people (mostly near-strangers) who say, "Oh, you should have kids. Children are so wonderful! You'll regret not having them! Women are having children well into their forties now. You should do it! There's still time."'

Even women who *have* children face judgement. Asti Mardiasmo-Povis says, 'I went through the fertility struggle and miscarriage. Now I have my daughter, Ariella, I am forever being asked when the second one is coming. When I say I am not sure whether there will be second one, people react with shock and horror, like I have committed a crime. And then I get the "wait until she's older, you'll want one then," or "don't wait – you're not getting any younger," and my favourite "you don't want it to be too late." Honestly, when I think about the questions and comments I used to get pre-Ariella and now post-Ariella, when am I going to win?'

Where does the judgement come from?

A common idea going around is that women who choose not to have kids are 'selfish'. Even women who might know better perpetuate the idea, such novelist Lionel Shriver, who, in 2005, penned an essay titled 'No kids please, we're selfish'.

Childfree adults are often depicted as self-involved people who sacrifice maternal bonds in order to go out partying, travel the world and spend money on materialistic possessions. In reality, this is often not the case. But, so what if it is? It is our choice how we spend our valuable time and money. Now, as my friends know, I do enjoy a nice bottle of Sauv or Veuve, but I do have obligations and responsibilities, too. They are just different to those of women who have children.

The idea that women don't have babies because they are 'selfish' is not only reductive, in many cases it is simply incorrect.

We are not the selfish ones. At least, we are no more selfish than those who *do* want kids.

How many childfree adults have heard their parents rant about when they are going to give them grandkids? The focus here is all about them wanting you to have a child for them! In what world is that the right thing to do?

Or how about parents, or people who want children, who say, 'I just want a mini me,' or 'I want a little boy who's just like my husband.' That reasoning is just as selfish as someone who chooses not to have children for personal reasons.

The word 'selfish' came up in many of the responses of people I have spoken to about this topic. Some women agreed that they didn't care to sacrifice their own pursuits, others pointed to the economic benefits of being childfree, and others objected strongly to the term. Many viewed raising a child as a significant choice, rather than simply what happens in the course of sex after marriage, and suggested that it was people who had children causally who were in fact selfish or irresponsible. As one woman wrote: 'People say it's "selfish" to not want to bring unwanted children into the world, but, to me, having children you don't want to have is much worse.'

We're not selfish. No one ever said, 'I really, *really* don't want to have a baby, but I›ll have one anyway, because it will make me a better person.' People have children because they want them, and those who choose to be childfree don›t. Yes, being a parent might involve you putting someone other than yourself first, but the decision to have that child was yours.

I say, 'screw you' to society. I will not accept your blame for the fall in population growth or feel bad for swimming against the tide. Why is it okay to impose on women the sole responsibility for population growth (or decline), to label a childfree woman as 'selfish', and then to insist that she just doesn't know what she's talking about and will eventually come around to a more rational line of thinking? I have never once sidled up to a group of mums watching their kids playing on the swing set and announced, 'One day, you'll change your mind.'

I empathise with women who want to be mothers and can't, but not desiring children does not make me selfish. And just because others might not understand my choice, it doesn't give them the right to ostracise, shame or manipulate me for that decision.

That is one of the keys to the issue right there – understanding others' choices. People, particularly other women, often don't understand the decision not to have children and, therefore, condemn it.

Interestingly, it's not only those of us who are childfree by choice who face judgement. During my research, I had countless women share their stories about being judged for having five kids, having IVF without a partner, only wanting one child and everything in between. Again, why should they be subject to judgement and ridicule?

Women like Donna, Mandy and Samantha are judged for having five kids. Samantha says it's taken her years of politeness to get to the point of bluntness when personal questions are thrown at her now. 'It's just rude. So now I respond in an equally personal way.'

SO LONG TO THE SISTERHOOD!

Interestingly, some of the biggest judgement comes from other women. In fact, it isn't just mums judging non-mums – they are judging each other, too. The conversation might be around a natural birth versus a C-section, breast versus bottle feeding, working versus staying at home, real versus disposable nappies, how many children you should or shouldn't have and so on.

Kate Hudson was recently blasted by a barrage of mums after she made comments about her C-section being the laziest thing she has ever done. Suddenly, women around the world jumped on the 'let's bash Kate' band wagon, with fellow C-section mums expressing their discontent on Twitter and Instagram.

'I've been a fan for a long time, but I was incredibly disappointed to read your comment regarding your C-section. How very inappropriate and insensitive,' wrote one commenter, while another wrote, 'Having my third C-section tomorrow. Don't feel lazy – just feel pissed at her.'

'Maybe if us C-section moms weren't made to feel like shit and less than moms for not giving birth vaginally, we could all just laugh this off as a bad joke,' added another. 'But here we are, with the "natural birth" community shaming us, and comments like this hurt those of us who had no choice.'

As Gwyneth Paltrow says, 'I never understand why mothers judge other mothers, like, "What do you mean you didn't breastfeed? What do you mean you didn't do this?" It's like, "Can't we all just be on each other's side?"'

As a childfree woman, I've felt like some mothers look down their nose at my life choice, somehow determining that they are superior to me. (These are the same ones who tell me that being a mother is the best job in the world and that I am missing out by not experiencing the love of a child.)

The judgement often comes in the form of verbal criticism or even exclusion from groups that are for 'mums only', and some common verbal barbs include: 'What would you know about kids? You're not a mother,' 'Those of us who have kids understand what true love is,' and 'You aren't a real woman unless you have children.'

I do get defensive about and resentful of this implied criticism that I am not a real woman. I would like to think it is not meant maliciously and maybe they are just curious about my life choice, but I think, often, it comes from their own fears and insecurities – just being projected onto me.

In fact, one of my old school friends sent me a direct Facebook message a few years ago preaching to me about my choice not to have children. Not only was I enraged by her barrage of messages, I was stunned by her belief that she had the right to tell me what to do with my life. She had no qualms in telling me what a big mistake I was making, how I would regret it, how I was missing out on so much and that I was basically living an empty life. I am not sure why she thought she had the right to preach to me about my life choices when I was perfectly happy.

I hear similar stories regularly. Kate says, 'I had an intern recently, a twenty-one-year-old Oxford graduate, who told me confidently she never wanted kids because it would get in the way of her career. I told her she was mad. While a childfree life looks fun on Facebook, no number of career highs, nights at the theatre, weekends away or adult pleasures can disguise the fact that it feels – there is no other word – empty.' I call bullshit.

Tracey Mathers, on the other hand, has been on the other end of women's judgement. 'I can't tell you the number of conversations I have had over the years where people have said things like, "Oh, you are one of those selfish ones always thinking of *you*," and that "I don't understand life because I don't have kids." I've also had plenty of people feel very sorry for me. I have been asked about medical conditions that are stopping me from having kids, told I must not feel complete, told I am a child hater, told I am missing out, told I am more like a man, and so much more.

'To me it is a very personal journey, one that is not an easy decision, and it's certainly gut wrenching if the decision has been take away from you. Luckily, I am a strong person, but people could really affect you with the hurtful things they say. I just want people to accept me for who and what I am, not be judged because I don't have children.'

I have been seriously shocked by some of the statements said to some of the women I interviewed for this book. Pressuring women to have children by trying to guilt them into it is the equivalent of bullying, and it is unacceptable.

Polite comments turn into intrusive ones very quickly.

I know there are plenty of women out there like me, with and without kids, who are sick of being judged for our choices. Donna Zen, a mother of five, says, 'I admire women who stand firm with their decision to not have children and tell their judgemental fold to just fuck off and mind their own business. Kids aren't for everyone and I don't believe you miss out on anything by not having them. Life is just different without them, not necessarily better or worse.'

Don't judge me on the choices I make about my body. Allow me to be my authentic self, just as I allow you to be. There is more than one way to live a life and be happy and fulfilled.

I, for one, would like women, and society in general, to focus on the positive, and stop judging and saying we are not real women because we defy our traditional roles. Start supporting the women around you for their choices, whether you agree with them or not.

We all face enough judgement as it is, and it's time for women to turn that judgement into support. It's time for a revolution, one that moves from feminism to fempowerment.

TAKE THE PRESSURE DOWN

I applaud anyone who truly wants to have a child, but I think it is very wrong to pressure anyone to do so. I have always and will always support my friends and families' decision to have children. As long as they are happy, that is all that matters to me. I don't care if they want ten children, to dye their hair purple or to live in Africa – it's their life and they can make the choices they want. I just want them to be happy.

I don't have to agree with them, just as they don't have to agree with me or approve of my life choices. It is not my place to judge or force my own opinions on them, nor should they be placing their judgements on me, or any other woman who chooses to be childfree.

So, let's lose the pressure and expectations, and create fairness and equality for all women, regardless of their choices. Mums shouldn't be rewarded for their life choices while childfree women are punished for theirs (even if only subconsciously). Everyone should be free to choose the life they want.

'Being a mum is incredibly challenging but we still feel a pressure to talk about it in very romantic terms. We all have that resentment at times and anxiety about being trapped by the role, that responsibility. And then chemically it can run riot... and there's no "off" button.'

CLAIRE DANES

THE MYTH OF MOTHERHOOD AND IDENTITY

Motherhood is an intrinsic part of our identity as women, or so we are told. As history has taught us, we are here to play a part and that is to be carer, nurturer and mother. That is role we are born into.

This is reinforced by the toys we are given, the stories we are read as children, the TV shows and movies we watch, what we are told in the media and how other people communicate with us. Even how governments identify and reward decisions to have children. There is no escaping the message of woman = mother.

Savvy Auntie founder *Melanie Notkin* shared some great insights into how motherhood is viewed in one of her recent blogs, 'Celebrating Others Day'. 'Hollywood moms and moms-to-be are celebrated and spotlighted with every baby-bump or rumoured baby-bump. Even actresses or reality TV stars many have never heard of headline websites with a photo and a caption as so-and-so "shows off" her pregnant belly. And childless stars are often asked in the media about when they'll become mothers, as if that's the missing piece to their overall success and happiness.'

This is what Notkin calls a media 'Mom-opia' – a myopic view of womanhood as motherhood. It's as if the W for woman was inverted to the M for mother, and every woman is seen through mother-coloured glasses.

At the other end of the spectrum, Notkin says, 'Childless women are often sidelined in the media as the frivolous "Carrie Bradshaw" type or the incomplete "Bridget Jones" type. The infantilisation of grown women who are childless by circumstance, by biology, or by choice can have the effect of feeling unnatural, left out or left behind, and of feeling less valuable in society.'

The reality of motherhood is far from the perfect world it is portrayed as. Side effects include, but are not limited to, weight gain, sleeplessness, incontinence, boredom, saggy breasts, depression, the end of romance, career downturn, loss of sex drive, poverty, exhaustion and a lack of fulfilment.

So why do so many see motherhood as an intrinsic part of a woman's identity?

We are taught that becoming mothers is essential to our identity from a young age. As we explored in an earlier chapter, we are given dolls as babies ourselves, given fairy tales to read, presented the right gendered toys to play with, and are educated by an outdated and bureaucratic system that essentially tries to bribe and brainwash women into believing it is their god given right to procreate, and for the good of their country and the world, they should.

This is further reinforced in movies, mummy blogs and the media, which portray being a mum as central to your identity as a woman. However, many mums struggle with transitioning from just being them to having a new life and identity overnight. How can you not struggle with this change in identity status? Your responsibilities are now very different. You go from being you to being mum. From being who you used to be to who you are now.

It makes sense in that you are trying to get back in control of your own life, a life that looks very different to what it used to. Your desires, motivations and spontaneous urges don't factor into your decision making as much as they used to. Now, you consider your children's needs equal to or above your own in the day to day.

THE RELATIONSHIP BETWEEN MOTHERHOOD AND IDENTITY

We are told our identity is built on our sacrifice to take care of other people. This is how society would like to show us a mother. But if we have friends or family with kids, the reality is vastly different.

Let's consider how motherhood is portrayed in the media.

Motherhood has been one of the biggest media fixations of the past few decades. We are sold this perfect mother ideal and stereotypes of mummy celebs, yummy mummies, irresponsible welfare mums, struggling single mums and everything in between.

Beginning in the late 1970s, the celebrity-mom profile spread like fire through popular women's magazines. The mum fairy tale is perpetuated with headlines like 'For me, happiness is having a baby', as Marie Osmond gushed on a 1983 cover of Good Housekeeping, and, as Linda Evans added in Ladies' Home Journal, 'All I want is a husband and baby.' (These ladies have a lot to answer for.)

Celebrities were presented as instruction manuals for how the rest of us should live our lives. Celebrity moms were perfect for the times and exemplified the materialism and elitism of the Reagan era balanced with the feminist dream of women being able to have a family and a job. And the media took full advantage of this with magazine editors figuring they could use stars to sell magazines and to serve as role models.

But has it gotten out of control? Celebrity moms are everywhere. The 'celeb mum' is celebrated through our culture, brandished on magazine covers, talked about on entertainment shows and put on a pedestal as the ultimate mum role model.

Stereotypical representations of women in the media is an issue, as the media defines roles and emphasizes stereotypes and helps to shape the cultural views of women. News media has the ability to set the agenda and infiltrate the thoughts of the public. Therefore, the media does not mirror reality, but rather constructs its own version of reality.

Constant representations of celebrity moms that perform to the impossibly high, media-generated standards of motherhood plague television, magazines, books and movies, stigmatizing working-class mothers. Unfortunately for women today, the media has an insatiable obsession with motherhood. But why?

Constant representations of super-moms in the media have raised the standards of motherhood to impossible ideals. Celebrity moms leverage consumerism at its finest, as they tout products in ads on TV, in blogs and in magazines, suggesting that children cannot be responsibly and effectively raised without expensive toys meant to stimulate their growing minds.

Commercialisation of the mum brand has spurned campaigns by companies like Dove, which launched Baby Dove, a set of products formulated for sensitive baby skin, and released a poignant video along with it. They're calling it the #RealMoms campaign, and they remind mothers everywhere that it's impossible to be perfect.

The video follows seven different moms who all face different challenges that affect the way they raise their kids. This video shows that motherhood doesn't look like any one thing. Any just about every variation is beautiful.

And let's not forget social media. In a recent New Parents Study by Sarah Schoppe-Sullivan, Professor of Human Sciences and Psychology at Ohio State University, they consider if Facebook may be fuelling new mothers' insecurity.

Schoppe -Sullivan says, 'We then tested whether Facebook use was associated with elevated depressive symptoms in the first months of parenthood. We found that mothers who were more prone to seek external validation for their mothering identity and were perfectionistic about parenting experienced increases in depressive symptoms indirectly through higher levels of Facebook activity. Moreover, greater Facebook activity was also linked to elevated parenting stress for new mothers.'

Stop comparing yourself to others' seemingly perfect images of parenting and life. All women, not just mums, who use Facebook and other social networking sites can help by sharing the struggles as well as the triumphs of parenting and life. They can also support instead of criticize mothers who portray themselves in a less-than-perfect but more authentic way.

A new process of media socialization needs to change the dialogue and the stereotypes should be removed from our contemporary vocabulary.

LOSING YOUR IDENTITY AS A MUM

While motherhood can be a big part of some women's identities, it can also be detrimental to others. For me, it would be like a massive chain around my neck. The obligation, expectation to be a perfect mother and loss of freedom would be like caging a wild animal.

Unsurprisingly, so many women lose themselves in motherhood. It is a like a silent war as they slowly fade away from themselves, their interests and their passions without even realising that it is happening. There is big transition that impacts their own personal growth once the baby is born.

There was one episode of Sex and the City titled 'The Baby Shower', where the four main characters (Carrie, Samantha, Miranda and Charlotte) attend the baby shower of their extroverted friend Laney, who is celebrating her pregnancy with her fellow suburban mums.

The girls arrive late after getting lost in the suburbs and one of the women remarks in a condescending voice not to remind her about her previous city life, as if her new life is so superior. The mums then gush over a baby basket like it's the second coming of Jesus, while Carrie, Samantha and Miranda watch in confusion, not knowing what all the fuss is about (meanwhile, Charlotte gets swept up in the baby buzz).

As Miranda so rightly points out, how can a woman with a Masters in Finance just want to talk about a diaper genie? (Whatever that is.)

I cringe when I watch Laney's excitement as she tears open bibs, bottles and breast pumps like they're pairs of designer shoes. (Yes, I get you need all this stuff for your new bub, but to me it's like getting excited about someone giving you a bottle of water.) And, later in the day, Laney comments about Samantha leading a sad, empty life going from bar hopping to bed hopping.

But underneath the bravado and superior attitude, Laney is struggling with dismay and heartbreak, revealing that she doesn't know what happened to her dreams, and she's secretly struggling with the change in her life.

I have never understood why, when smart women have children, they can't continue to have conversations about things other than their children. We've all been at those lunches or dinners when the topic starts with, continues with and ends with one thing – their kids!

As a friend, yes, I want to know what is happening in my friend's life (even if she happens to be a new mum). But her kids are just one part of that life. What happened to everything else?

Take Renee, who didn't personally want children but decided to have them because her husband did. She found that, while she doesn't regret the decision, it did have a big impact on her identity. 'Having a child has been the best thing and worst thing I've done. I had a minor identity crisis to start with – no more drinking, no more smoking. I lost a lot of friends then we moved and I was further isolated. It's been a tough trot but I wouldn't trade it for anything. I am still trying to figure out who I am because much of my identity is being a mum, but I don't identify as one.'

I have seen so many women lose themselves when they become mothers because they are so wrapped up in their kids. Some mothers totally change their lives, and sometimes who they are, after they have children. Before you start to scream, 'Of course you need to change your life!' understand my perspective for just a minute.

I believe kids should fit into your life, not the other way around. I remember my parents playing tennis with their friends one night a week in summer and we would go along in our PJs and sleep in the car at bedtime. It certainly didn't hurt us and I know I enjoyed the novelty of it. I don't recall them saying, 'We can't go because the kids have to be asleep at 8pm.'

In her blog from 'A Mother Far from Home', Rachel Norman shares why women lose their identity post child. As a mum to five kids in five years, I think she is well qualified to speak about this very topic.

She feels there are several reasons why women lose their identity. The focus is now on the child, not you, and your life revolves around them. Many women stop caring about how they look, as time becomes a luxury they can no longer afford. Their old identity perhaps revolved around their job or career and this is no longer the case. They have lost the freedoms they once enjoyed day to day. And, lastly, she says they just don't get enough sleep.

Ex First Lady Michelle Obama had a great quote around motherhood and identity: 'I'm Not a Mother First. Women need to put personhood before parenthood.'

Identifying as a mom means that women are expected to be everything and give up anything for their children. But women can separate themselves from 'motherhood' and still remain good mothers and women. The two are not and should not be intertwined.

Why is it so easy for women to lose themselves as mothers? You can still be yourself and be a mum. The two can co-exist if you want them to. Again, it is all about choice!

It's understandable that some women would embrace motherhood as their primary and most important identity. Yes, we are mothers and sisters and daughters and wives. We're also much more. And declaring our individual importance as woman does not diminish the depth of love we have for our children or the central role parent-hood plays in our lives.

Forty-year-old Kirsty Anya Le Jeune doesn't define herself just as a mother. 'I am multiple things, I'm a mum, a business woman, a woman, a horse woman, a daughter, a friend, not anyone ahead of the other but all things at once. I think that we are mentors to our children, and being passionate and living fully teaches them to also.'

On the other side of this is thirty-one-year-old Katie Aquelina, who has upended her whole identity to fit around her new role as a mum. 'I thought I always wanted to be a Mum and found myself pregnant unexpectedly around the time we were going to start try-ing anyway. While pregnant I was very aware of how my life would be completely altered and was very anxious about "loosing me". Our son entered the world under tough circumstances (medically) and I had a rough start into motherhood so it really brought home the fact that he (my son) should be the priority in my life, especially being the primary carer. I quit my job, changed careers to allow me to stay home until he (and now my daughter) was at school. My whole life now revolves around providing what they need first and foremost and everything else is secondary. I feel that having Archer's issue around birth and him having a short stay in special care changed my whole perspective on being a Mum, whereas if everything had gone smoothly I may have taken it for granted and tried to continue on with my lifestyle prior to becoming a Mum.'

New mums-to-be are often told that nothing from your pre-baby life will matter once the baby is born. But it should and it does, as this is what has made you who you are as a woman.

And let's not forget being wives and lovers to our partners, which is just as important to our identity as women. Regardless of being a mum or not, I think, as women, we should not limit ourselves to one label when we are so much more than that.

Shouldn't you be enough for you? Why do you need anyone to complete you? And I include men in that statement – I love my husband but I don't need him to complete me. I am more than enough, as he will likely agree. I am sometimes too much!

I am certainly not alone in my opinion. As actress Marisa Tomei said in an interview with Manhattan Magazine, 'I'm not that big a fan of marriage as an institution, and I don't know why women need to have children to be seen as complete human beings.'

Motherhood is the cultural norm but contemporary womanhood is offering equally valuable and viable alternatives.

TO BE ME, OR NOT TO BE ME

One of my dear friends, Darlene, has four children. In this world of self-indulged, spoilt, little brats (yes, I said it), these are four of the best-behaved children you will find. They are disciplined, respectful, take responsibility and have good values. They are also encouraged to follow their passions, to be the best they can be and to shine as individuals. I have a lot of admiration for Darlene and her husband Adam. Actually, I have a lot of admiration for anyone who can raise balanced, polite and well-behaved kids in today's world.

However, what I also greatly admire about Darlene is the fact that she hasn't let having four children hold her back from what she wants to achieve in life. With her four kids, Darlene still has a full-time job as a teacher's aide, she gets up several mornings a week to do a seven- to ten-kilometre run, she has run two half-marathons, and she juggles this with being a wife and running four kids to soccer practice, dance lessons, guitar lessons and everything in between. Did I mention she's also recovering from Ross River Fever? That is why I call her Wonder Woman!

By contrast, I see so many women letting their kids stop them from living the lives they want. I remember, one day, my sister was complaining about being overweight, so I told her to stop complaining and do something about it. She replied, 'I've got three kids, you know.' You can guess what my response was...

It's time we started to separate the terms 'woman' and 'mother'. Being a mother is an extension of being a woman if that is what you choose, however, it is not the definition of it.

Whether you have kids or not, this shouldn't be the basis for your identity. You are not incomplete if you don't have children. And if you do have children, they shouldn't be all that you are. You can be a mum but not define yourself in that way. It's important to hold on to who you really are – so you can still be the best version of yourself *as well as* being a mother, rather than having to choose between being that best version of yourself *or* being a mother.

As women, we have traditionally been defined as: *husband + child = woman.* I say, let's change the equation to: *me + choice = woman.*

'My desire to reproduce is actually getting less and less as I get older, which is starting to worry me. I was keen on having a child in my early twenties, but that enthusiasm has waned over time.'

JENNIFER LAWRENCE

TICK TOCK GOES THE BIOLOGICAL CLOCK (OR DOES IT?)

I keep hearing stories about this thing called the biological clock. In *The Women,* Meg Ryan's character, Mary, describes feeling the tug of her uterus, and how she might be thinking about having another baby, 'since I know the gate's closing.'

Well, my biological clock has never ticked. It's not even stuck on permanent snooze – it just has no batteries. I have never had any biological urges nor have I felt an evolutionary drive to procreate (just because I can).

When I see articles written by bloggers and journalists on the topic of a woman's biological clock, there is an assumption that every woman feels a hormonal urge to procreate and that she is feeling an emotional pull over this desire. That's a big assumption to make.

So, where did the biological clock come from? If not all women feel it, is it even real? And for those of us who do feel it, how do we know if we genuinely want to have kids, or if it's just our hormones making themselves heard?

In this chapter, I'll share the origins of the biological clock, as well as what really drives the urge (believe it or not, it isn't biology!).

THE BIRTH OF THE BIOLOGICAL CLOCK

Theories about female sexuality, maternal instincts and the biological clock have developed in abundance over the last two hundred years.

The concept of maternal instinct has figured prominently in scientific theories since the time of Charles Darwin. Around the turn of the nineteenth century, men were wrenched away from daily life in the home, which morphed in to a 'domestic sphere' inhabited by a mother and her children. It is during this historical moment that a familial myth was born: maternal instinct. The Industrial Revolution's new division of responsibility necessitated a reconfiguration of the family unit, and Western cultures had to adapt. So, they retrofitted special traits onto women, who were now exclusively responsible for raising children. These women, the incipient myth suggested, were biologically hardwired to rear children. It was this gendered instinct that made them uniquely suited to their new role as a family's sole caretaker.

It wasn't surprising that, by the late nineteenth-century, psychologists believed women possessed a unique need to create and care for offspring. In the late 1800s, experts attempted to use biology to shore up this theory, positing that maternal instinct was located in the female reproductive organs.

Then, in the early twentieth century, psychologist Sigmund Freud developed theories around female sexuality. Like the early sexologists, Freud believed that women were sexually passive, engaging in sex only because they wanted children. He also believed that we suffered from penis envy – he believed girls felt anxiety upon realising they did not have a penis, and then experienced sexual desire towards men and an urge to have male children in an attempt to gain a penis. Penis envy in women is a problem that Freud believed could never be completely resolved, implying that women would always be morally inferior to men, who were capable of having fully developed superegos because of their biological sex.

At the same time, for hundreds of years, women had been diagnosed with hysteria – a disorder that exhibited the symptoms of faintness, nervousness, sexual desire, insomnia, fluid retention, a loss of appetite for food or sex and, interestingly, a tendency to cause trouble. The disorder was believed to be related to the woman's uterus – the original theories posited women had a wandering womb (which was believed to literally travel around the body causing problems), while later theories centred on the uterus producing its own form of semen, and hysteria being caused by that semen being retained for too long. By the mid-nineteenth century, it was believed that a quarter of all women suffered from hysteria.

The cure for hysteria up until the twentieth century was masturbation, which has been linked to the development of the vibrator – an 'electro-mechanical medical instrument' providing more reliable and efficient physical therapy for women believed to be suffering from hysteria.

What's interesting is that, wherever you look throughout history, most of the definitions and theories around female sexuality were created by men, and many of them still influence our thoughts and actions today.

Consider the biological clock – a concept that was first referred to in the Washington Post in 1978. Sometimes referred to as 'baby panic', it wasn't a term coined by a scientist, or a woman describing her own experience of having an obsession with having children 'kick in'. Rather, it was created by the writer Richard Cohen, who, in a piece about how women were managing jobs and family, noted that 'the clock is ticking for the career woman.'

Meanwhile, in an interview with author Gabrielle Moss, Jenna Healey at Yale University's Institution for Social and Political Studies stated that the phrase was introduced to the general public at the same time in vitro fertilisation (IVF) was becoming publicly available, with the two concepts being 'inextricably linked in the public mind'.

This may have influenced people to associate the phrase 'biological clock' with the idea of a woman who is extremely eager to conceive, rather than the reality of simply outlining the timeframe in which pregnancy can occur.

Today, the media continues to reinforce the social norm of motherhood by constantly reminding women of their 'ticking biological clock'. In a *Psychology Today* article published in 2013, evolutionary psychologist Gillian Ragsdale noted that 'the press is awash with warnings about delaying motherhood and the short-sighted selfishness of career-hungry women who suddenly realise it›s now or never. The implication is that either these women have been suppressing their maternal drive in pursuit of other rewards, or they never had any.'

An article by Melanie Berliet, American author and journalist, entitled *It's Time to Stop Bullying 30-Something Women about Their Biological Clocks,* talks about the fact that thirty-something women are constantly bombarded with infertility horror stories, urban legends and stories sharing anecdotal evidence intended to demonstrate that if you wait too long, you're destined to get screwed over by Mother Nature.

She states, 'We're shamed into believing that our limited supply of eggs might soon be entirely worthless, and urged to consider egg freezing, an intensive procedure that costs an astounding $10,000 on average, "just in case."'

THE TRUTH BEHIND THE THEORY

So, is there any truth behind the idea of a biological clock?

While there's no 'magic number' at which female fertility declines, eggs do deteriorate with age, says Infertility Network UK's deputy chief executive Susan Seenan. 'The speed of that deterioration will vary but rises more steeply after the age of about thirty-five. The more "fertility aware" you are the better, so you can make an informed decision and be aware that it might take you longer to conceive.'

In Britain, the NHS agrees that *thirty-five is a key age* when it comes to female fertility. Women are most fertile in their early twenties and their fertility declines with age. From the age of thirty-five, this fall becomes steeper.

So, what is actually happening on a biological level?

Women are born with all the eggs they will ever have. As a woman ages, her eggs age with her, diminishing in quantity and quality. It then takes longer to conceive and the risk of not being able to get pregnant increases. Starting at about age thirty-two, a woman's chances of conceiving decrease gradually but significantly. From age thirty-five, the fertility decline speeds up. At thirty, the chance of conceiving each month is about twenty per cent. At forty, it's around five per cent and fertility has fallen by fifty per cent.

Beyond the issue of fertility, though, there are more pregnancy and birth risks for older mothers, including miscarriage, still birth, birth complications, gestational diabetes, placenta praevia and placenta abruption. (I won't pretend to know what those things actually are, but they don't sound good.) A woman over thirty-five is nearly 2.5 times more likely than a younger woman to have a stillbirth. By age forty, she is more than five times more likely to have a stillbirth than a woman under thirty-five. For a woman aged forty, the risk of miscarriage is greater than the chance of a live birth. If an older women does have a child, she is also more likely to have a baby with birth defects or genetic abnormalities.

Interestingly, the father's age can also impact on chance of conception, time to pregnancy, risk of miscarriage and the health of the child, though we rarely hear the media talking about fertility from that perspective!

Age also affects the success of IVF, with IVF Australia saying that the success rate is 40.1 per cent per embryo transfer leading to a live birth for patients under thirty years, but only 8.5 per cent per embryo transfer leading to a live birth for patients over forty years.

At the same time, the average age of women using IVF has increased. Data from studies carried out by the Australian Institute of Health and Welfare reveals that, in 2012, the average age of women receiving treatment using their own eggs or embryos was thirty-six years, while the average age for women using donated eggs or embryos was 40.8 years. In 2014, the average age of women having IVF treatment remained at thirty-six years, which is almost six years older the average age of women giving birth in Australia.

Commenting on her experience, forty-two-year-old Selina Box Mc-Callum wishes she had not left having children so late. She says, 'IVF is certainly something I don't recommend if you can avoid it. I would encourage women to put their eggs on ice after the age of thirty-five if they haven't met their partner, just aren't ready or think they might change their mind. Sometimes we think we have a choice until it's too late then we don't have a choice anymore.

'I wish I knew how hard it would be to fall pregnant after thirty-five. I have friends who are doctors who didn't want to have kids then changed their mind in their late-thirties but, after trying for four years, still cannot conceive. It's been devastating for them. In the past when I thought people should just mind their business, now I see that maybe they weren't judging but just offering some advice and leaving it up to me to make a choice. For me personally, I wish I'd had someone butt in and tell me, "Hey, do you realise that your chances of falling pregnant are significantly reduced after thirty-five?"'

Age is not something we can control. But if you want a baby, and you're in a relationship, you can have a conversation with your partner sooner rather than later.

THERE'S NO SUCH THING AS THE BIOLOGICAL CLOCK

While there is some truth around fertility and age, how does that stack up against the theory of the biological clock, or the idea that all women have a biological urge to become mothers?

The term 'biological urge' refers to when a woman experiences an uncontrollable feeling that she needs to become a mother. It's seen as part of women's biological instinct to have children. But what do we actually mean by the term 'instinct'? The 1961 edited volume *Instinct* laid down some defining guidelines: To qualify as an instinct, the behaviour should be automatic, irresistible, triggered by something in the *environment,* occur at some particular time during development, require no training, be unmodifiable and occur in all individuals of a species.

So few human behaviours are qualified as 'instincts' that psychologists have replaced the term with 'drives'. The idea is that we have a set of innate drives that pushes our behaviour in pre-set directions. Drives are innate, they are not learned, and (with occasional exceptions) they are universal. We all have them.

So, how does this stack up against the idea of a biological clock?

As far back as the early 1900s, women were contesting the existence of a biological clock. An article published in a 1916 issue of the American Journal of Sociology by psychologist Leta Hollingworth challenges the widespread myth of maternal desire as being intense and innate in all women. She thought interest in having children naturally varied from those with 'zero or negative interest' through to those with a moderate amount of interest to those whose 'only vocational or personal interest lies in maternal activities'.

Ultimately, she concluded that 'there is no verifiable evidence to show that a maternal instinct exists in women of such all-consuming strength and fervour as to impel them voluntarily to seek the pain, danger, and exacting labour involved in maintaining a high birth rate.'

100 years later, an article written by Gabrielle Moss in 2016 on this very topic suggests that there is no such thing as the biological clock. There has not been a single study that has confirmed the existence of a scientific, hormonal urge that causes women to help-lessly desire children.

If the biological clock exists, why do one in four women choose not to have kids? Why do so many of us use birth control to prevent pregnancies, including those women who *want* kids, but maybe not yet, or maybe no more than they already have?

Birth control has been around since ancient times. Ancient Egyptian women used a combination of cotton, dates, honey and acacia as a suppository, and it turns out fermented acacia really does have a spermicidal effect. The Bible and the Koran both refer to **coitus interruptus** (the withdrawal method). The pill was then approved for contraceptive use in 1960 (though it was controversial, with the Pope openly denouncing its use).

Fast forward to today and we have many choices open to us, start-ing with 'protect as you go' methods like condoms (male or female), the cervical cap, the diaphragm and spermicides. There are then more reliable options, like the contraceptive pill; Implanon, which is implanted into your arm; NuvaRing, which is inserted into the vagina like a tampon, where it releases a steady amount of estrogen and progestin throughout the month; and Ortho Evra, which is a skin patch with hormones embedded in its adhesive layer. Plus, let's not forget the Mirena, Kyleena and Skyla, which are intrauterine devices (IUDs) that continuously release a progestin called levonorgestrel.

Or you can choose a permanent option, like a vasectomy for men, tubal ligation for women and a new, less invasive, nonsurgical option for women known by its brand name, Essure. The nonsurgical procedure can be done in your doctor's office in about thirty minutes with only a local anaesthetic. During the procedure, your doctor uses a special instrument called a hysteroscope to place an insert through your vagina and cervix and into the opening of your fallopian tube in your uterus. Within three months, the insert causes your body to form a tissue barrier that prevents sperm from reaching the egg.

Having said that, sometimes, permanent birth control is easier to access in theory than it is in practice.

Christen Reighter spoke in a TEDx Talk about her experience of being surgically sterilised, and the condescending and dismissive nature of the doctors she met with, all of whom considered her to be too young, or said that she would change her mind. In the talk, you can see she was visibly upset by her experience, yet, determined to get these medical professionals to understand that she was making a very informed decision that she had not only thought long and hard about, but had extensively researched to determine the pros and cons. It was a decision not taken lightly by her or by the many other women who had had the same experience and been refused treatment.

Often, there is no real medical reason for being refused such a treatment. Instead, decisions seem to be based on the fact a woman is young and will regret the decision later in life, or the belief she doesn't really understand what she is doing.

The regret argument doesn't fly with me. Life can be full of regrets – I could regret buying a certain car, choosing to be a lawyer, spending $800 on a pair of Jimmy Choo's, or taking a new job I hated. And who's to say you won't regret having children? It's disappointing that medical professionals can make these judgements about any educated woman who has made the decision not to have children, yet, any teenage girl is free to get herself pregnant with no thought whatsoever.

I am vehemently pro-choice and believe no one has the right to tell a woman what to do, in any circumstances. Unless you walk a mile in her shoes, you do not know someone's circumstances or reasons for their choices, so telling someone who has a put a lot of thought into a major, life-changing decision like having her tubes tied that she doesn't know her own mind is highly offensive.

Women today have at least seventeen forms of contraception available to them, with several of these options preventing STIs along with preventing pregnancy.

With so many women choosing to be childfree, isn't that evidence enough that the biological clock doesn't actually exist and this feeling is, in fact, a by-product of society's brainwashing over many years?

The same goes for the related concept 'baby fever'. Husband and wife research team Gary and Sandra Brase started with a formal survey designed to figure out if baby fever actually exists. They learned that both men and women can develop it, although its intensity varies from person to person and within the same person over time. 'Baby fever is normal, it varies a lot, and people don't have to feel it,' says Gary Brase, associate professor of psychology at Kansas State University.

The researchers also looked at three potential explanations for baby fever: the sociocultural view, the by-product view and the adaptationist view.

According to the sociocultural view, people – especially women – are acculturated to crave babies. 'People might think they want to have children because they are supposed to have children,' says Brase. Brase and his wife asked eighty college students of varying ages to rate how frequently they had a desire to have children, then administered a test that assessed how strongly they affiliated with particular gender roles. After sorting the data, they found that the sociocultural view was 'not a great predictor of how strongly people felt a desire to have children.'

The by-product view holds that people want to have children to fulfil an urge to nurture. But the Brases found that this theory didn't tell the whole story either.

The Brases haven't looked in depth at how people's baby-lust evolves once they have children. But they have noticed that women's average baby-fever rating went down after they had children, while men's went up. What gives? 'I have noticed the change in my own desire after I had kids,' says Brase. 'Babies were more attractive and I wanted to hold them.'

Finally, the Brases trained their lens on the adaptationist view, which theorises that baby fever is an emotional signal that subconsciously hints to the brain that it might be a good time to have a baby. When testing out this hypothesis, the Brases found that positive exposure to babies made people want to have kids, while negative exposure (crying, stinky infants) made people shy away from the idea of parenthood. 'People's desire to have children is most influenced by the positive and negative interactions and the trade-offs,' Brase concludes.

While the biological clock and baby fever aren't universal biological urges, there are many women for whom the urge is real.

Kate Brimfield said she certainly did feel the tick of the biological clock. 'With all my health issues, my IVF doctor in Queensland told me that if I didn't have children by the time I was thirty-five I would never have them. Leading up to that, I definitely felt the clock ticking.

'We didn't realise anything was wrong with my health until we started trying to get pregnant and I discovered I had a condition called PCOS (polycystic ovarian syndrome), which would affect my chances of getting pregnant. We saw a specialist in Melbourne who told us to just keep trying. But, after being put on a drug called Clomid for a year and making no progress, I knew there was something more impacting my ability to get pregnant. Then I discovered I had severe endometriosis and both my fallopian tubes were blocked and would need to be removed, which meant IVF was our only chance of having children.

'Fast forward to August 4th 2016 and I finally got to meet my little miracle after thirteen years of trying, lots of tears, heartbreak and laughter. Flynn Raymond Brimfield made his way into this world completing our little family. The chances of me being able to have another child is one in a million, but we are happy with our little miracle.'

Some women feel the tick tock unexpectedly, like Diana. 'I was always quite adamant that I didn't want children and maintained this stance until I was thirty-one. Upon meeting the "right" partner to have a family with, it seems my biological clock kicked in and I instantly had a need to start a family.

'We did many rounds of IVF and even tried a donor egg program in the US, which was guaranteed or your money back. All up I think we paid over $200,000 in our attempts to have a baby. We became resigned to the fact that we weren't going to be parents and I sought out friendships with women who were childfree.'

Meanwhile, Nikki says, 'In my early- to mid-twenties, I was ambivalent about having children. I was not massively for, but not against either. I guess I just always assumed I would. As I hit my late-twenties and my close friends started having children, the urge started to come on quite strong. I struggled in the relationship-department, so I started to tell myself I would go "Single Mother by Choice" if the years ticked by and I didn't have strong prospects on the scene.

'I got engaged in my early thirties, which I can see in hindsight was 100 per cent biology-driven. This man was strong, ambitious, successful – all the biological traits that equal a good father and provider. But I could see that he was ambivalent at best, if not opposed, to having children. So I left the relationship. With the benefit of hindsight, I can see that he was *so* not a good partner for me.

'No wonder my relationships weren't successful – I had been meeting men and looking at them as sperm-donors; not necessarily people I would like to spend time (let alone the rest of my life!) with.'

Similarly, after not wanting children when she was younger, Jae's biological clock switched on at twenty-nine. 'Everyone knew I never wanted marriage or kids. But I met my now husband when I was twenty-five, and at twenty-nine the urge hit me like a ton of bricks. My biological clock started ticking so fucking loudly that I simply couldn't ignore it. I just had to have a baby. So I did.'

As Danielle Friedman reported in *The Daily Beast,* 'Many scientists believe the seemingly biological drive some women feel isn't triggered by biology, so much as culture,' and that according to evolutionary biologists, 'Evolution has bestowed upon women a desire for sex and the equipment to have a baby; from here, free will steps in.'

And this isn't surprising, with the overwhelming focus on motherhood that surrounds us. Just think of passing comments from friends and family, the prevalence of motherhood in the media, and the fact that, for most of us, the person who largely modelled what it meant to be a woman to us was our own mother.

The narrative around a biological clock and failing fertility just adds fuel to the fire. As Melanie Berliet writes, 'We caution young ladies that if they wait to procreate, they'll face devastating setbacks down the line. We tell them that their bodies were built to carry babies sooner rather than later (i.e. now!). We say there's "never a right time" to have a child, as if women should drop everything and get preggers regardless of how prepared they actually feel, financially, emotionally, or otherwise.'

However, all of this raises the question: 'If the "right time" never arrives, is it so crazy to presume that a woman might not be cut out for motherhood after all?'

JUST BECAUSE YOU CAN HAVE KIDS, DOESN'T MEAN YOU SHOULD

Just because you are biologically capable of having a child, it doesn't mean you should have to choose to have children or want that path for your life.

I know I'm biologically capable of running a marathon, sleeping four hours a night or eating a massive bag of potato chips. That does not mean I want to or choose to do any of those things. But if *you* want to do those things, go ahead. It is your life and your choice. The same is true for whether or not you have a child.

Not having a child impacts one person (yourself), however, having a child when you don't want one impacts you, the child and their development, the father and perhaps your society and taxpayers if you decide you don't want that child and it becomes a burden on the system. Why gamble with a human life?

The desire to have children is not innate. Many women have never wanted to experience giving birth. And that's okay. If you want to experience driving along the Amalfi coast, eating in an underwater restaurant, making great art, having a passionate love affair, or going to an airport and jumping on the next plane, do *that!*

'I'd be a terrible father. I see my friends who have children and I'm like, "Dude, how are you even upright, much less here at work at 6am?"'

JON HAMM

LET'S NOT FORGET THE BLOKES!

With all of this discussion on the different elements influencing women to have children, it can be easy to forget about the men in our lives.

Times are changing. These days, in many households, women earn more than men. Men are allowed to take paternity leave. Both men and women struggle with the roles of 'homemaker' and 'provider'. Both roles have changed significantly over the decades. The expectation that woman should want children is the equivalent of saying all men should want to drink beer.

Author of *The Masculine Mystique,* Stephen Marches, writes, 'The days of dad working all week and then, having fulfilled his duties, going to play two or three rounds of golf on the weekend are long gone. Instead, husbands are often expected to be fully involved in raising the children and housework, while simultaneously remaining the main financial provider. And, by taking on the role as the financial provider during the marriage, if a marriage breaks down, many husbands find they have unwittingly put themselves in a position to continue this role whether they want to or not.'

Perhaps not all men want to be providers, just like not all women want to be caretakers?

The question of having kids is a big one that can drive many couples apart. Conventional wisdom would cast this as a baby-hungry woman up against a skittish man, but in some relationships, it is the exact opposite.

So, what do men really want?

WHAT MEN WANT

In a *nationally representative survey* of single, childless people in 2011, more men than women said they wanted kids. On the other hand, more women reported seeking independence in their relationships, personal space, interests and hobbies. A USA Today survey in 2013 echoed those findings, with more than eighty per cent of men saying they'd always wanted to be a father or at least thought they would be someday. Just seventy per cent of women felt the same.

So, why are men so keen to settle down and have kids?

For some men, it is the desire to experience the ultimate form of self-discovery, to produce a child who reflects everything about them. One guy mentioned that he felt growing old without ever procreating to be a type of life failure. 'Having a kid is a marker of success,' he said, 'along with owning a chunk of land and having a certain amount of money.' He admitted this view treated children as a kind of 'bourgeois accessory', but explained he can't help it – it's an attitude he inherited from his prolifically populating family.

Another said, 'I fear waking up when I'm in my mid-forties having had a successful professional life, but without kids. I don't want to be left out. I don't want the music to stop and for me to be the only one without a chair.'

And from a mid-thirties guy who had spent his life travelling, establishing his career and partying: 'Most of what I wanted to do was get drunk and have a good time. But after seventeen years of that I thought, "Is this it? Is this what I'm living for?" My life was all about meeting my hedonic needs and I decided there has to be something more.'

Armin Brott, one of the forefathers of fatherhood thinking, who has authored eight books on the subject, says he's noticed a distinction between male and female fantasies about parenthood. 'Generally, women will think about taking care of a completely newborn baby, but men skip ahead a few years to playing catch, reading and talking, showing the kid how to fly a kite.'

For men and women, a lot of the reasons for wanting and not wanting children are very similar, however, it seems that woman are the ones who are thinking twice before jumping on the mum train.

Today's young women have more of a choice about their fertility than their grandmothers did, and perhaps clearer eyes about the challenges of child-rearing than their mothers. For these women's grandparents, having children wasn't a question, it was a given. And they had lots of them, spawning the baby-boom generation: The birth rate *reached 122.7 children* born per 1,000 women of childbearing age in 1957. Boomers themselves had more of a choice thanks to the widespread adoption of the pill and changing social expectations brought on by the women's liberation movement, and the birth rate sagged, then stabilised.

This leaves more and more women choosing to pursue other things in life – careers, travel and hobbies – while more men want children. Believe it or not, **men** are actually the ones who are eager to settle down and reproduce, while women are hesitant, as discussed in a recent piece by Bryce Covert in New York Magazine's *'The Cut'*.

Darlene (the mother of four I mentioned earlier) says her husband wanted a tribe of kids and would've happily had more if her body had allowed.

MEN WHO CHOOSE TO BE CHILDFREE

Even though there is a large number of men who want children, the childfree contingent is still running strong. Luckily for them, childfree men haven't shared the barrage of attacks their female counterparts have endured since the advent of birth control.

Just consider when I asked my husband Shayne if the 'kid conversation' was ever mentioned at his work. Did the guys ask him about having children? His response was, 'It's probably been mentioned when I started and when you say we don't have kids by choice, that's the end of it – conversation over. We're not like you women who judge one another. For us it's not a big deal. We answer then move on.'

(As a side note, how do men without children get off so much easier? Or do they? I recently saw an article online titled *'Childless Men May Face Higher Risk of Heart Disease',* so I guess we're all screwed!)

So why do men choose to be childfree?

An article for The Good Men Project found that while women face more stigma, both genders give the same reasons for not having kids. The top four reasons, which are the same among men and women, are:

1. 'I love our life, our relationship, as it is, and having a child won't enhance it.'
2. 'I do not want to take on the responsibility of raising a child.'

3. 'I have no desire to have a child, no maternal or paternal instinct.'

4. 'I want to accomplish things in life that would be difficult if I were a parent.'

One man noted, 'Why be a responsible dad when you can be a cool uncle?'

A survey conducted by author Laura S. Scott, author of **Two is Enough: A Couple's Guide to Living Childless by Choice**, found that men and women's reasons for choosing blissfully unladen lives are basically the same. The men she interviewed range from twenty-six to fifty-three, and hail from the US, Canada and Australia. Their answers to this survey about why men don't want to have children may or may not surprise you, but what they unquestionably do is give you a glimpse of the men's world in a way you haven't seen it before.

Erich, twenty-seven, Canada: 'I want the freedom to travel, to work wherever I want, to come and go as I please. I want the freedom to have freedom. Can't just pick up and go with a kid.'

Alan Smith, fifty-three, Brisbane: 'I actually find this a difficult question to comprehend. For me, the opposite question applies, "Why on earth would anyone *wish* to produce children?" I do realise that people have children for all sorts of reasons – they find them endearing, they feel they have a religious or social duty to breed, the vanity of having a copy of themselves, a need to prove their "manhood" or "womanhood", the financial benefits or simply that they have never thought about it and regarded it as a "default" position to reproduce. None of these applies to me.'

Josh, thirty-six, Oklahoma: 'I like the freedom. I'm the type of person who needs a lot of downtime, and a child would definitely get in the way of that. I also just don't like being completely responsible for something other than myself. I have no more desire to have a pet than I do to have a kid.'

Anonymous, twenty-six, Montana: 'For me, it was a bit of knowing my nature. I can be overly caring and take things a bit personally. If I had a child, I would imagine that I'd feel I let them down greatly if they failed at something. In the same breath, when I put my mind to accomplishing a goal, I block out everything around me until I finish my goal. I didn't want to live a life that was both unfair to that child and to me. I would probably drive the child nuts and cause a mini hell for myself. Once I add in the fact I'd probably have a partner in the mix, it seems very maddening.'

When asked if they had ever been judged for not wanting children, their answers were similar to women who have made the same choice, and some found they were labelled as playboys, irresponsible and commitment phobic.

Erich: 'The most common judgment is that I'm "selfish" (i.e. just want to be promiscuous). Mostly from people who finished whatever schooling they started and bought into the white picket fence routine of life and never considered there were alternatives.'

Alan: 'Frequently – by (a) the media, who seem to regard breeding as a heroic act, (b) by politicians, who are obsessed with "the family" and regard childless or childfree adults as "non-people," (c) by the taxation and economic systems that discriminate against me, (d) by the advertising media that seem to assume everyone is a member of a "mum-dad-2.3-kids nuclear family," (e) by the occasional jealous breeder, and (f) by religious fanatics who regard sex when not utilised for procreation as against God's directive.'

And, like women, men who want to be childfree but end up having children anyway may regret the experience. Take this father from Florida, who had the courage to share his honest view about becoming a father in *Men's Health Forum* in 2011.

'I was always hesitant to have children; it wasn't something I really "wanted". My wife and I waited for about five years after marriage to finally bite the bullet and get pregnant. It was well planned and went off without a hitch. It basically came down to "if we're going to have kids, we need to do it soon so they can be gone by the time I'm wanting to retire." It's now four years further down the road, my daughter is three, and we've just had a son. We agree that we're done, and now it's time for me to get the big snip.

'Unfortunately, having the second child has only exacerbated feelings I have had pent up for a while, namely that of not wanting to be a father. I fully realise it's far too late for that and I'm basically whining like a little puppy, but the fact remains that I feel as if I am watching the best years of my life wash away and I'm not spending them in a productive or satisfying way.

'I estimate that about twenty per cent of the time the family is something I enjoy, ten per cent of the time is neutral, and the remaining seventy per cent is time I really dislike it. I would like to get somewhere closer to sixty per cent enjoyment; however, I seem to be trending in the wrong direction. I have noticed I've become less patient with my daughter, and my son is about a month old so pretty much all I feel for him is some dislike rising from the amount of attention he requires.

'Many seem to feel that the big payoff of parenting is when the children become young adults. Being a natural defensive pessimist, I find it difficult to look forward to this highly speculative future, lest I be severely disappointed when it doesn't materialise.

'In many ways I feel trapped, and I have no one to blame but myself. I was the one who decided to propose marriage, I agreed to have children, and now I am the one who has to live with his increasingly negative feelings about his family. I hardly spend any time alone, or with friends, so I feel I have no release and these emotions are just bottling up (I have a terrible history of this, it runs in the family). I would like to ask for advice, but in the past the advice offered has been of the magnitude of "Just cheer up," "It's not about you," "You made the bed, now lie in it," "You'll enjoy them when they're older."

'I have considered divorce, but I pretty much stand to lose everything and gain nothing (which would do wonders for my already bleak outlook on life in general). So perhaps rather than offer advice, just let me vent a little and use this forum as a kind of release.'

I think the moral of the story is that, whether you're a woman or a man, you need to make the decision for the right reasons. If not, you could find yourself facing a long life of regret.

IT TAKES TWO TO TANGO – COMMUNICATING YOUR WANTS

I've already shared that, when I met Shayne, my attitude was one of 'I don't want a boyfriend, I don't want anything serious.' It didn't take me long before I realised how special he was, at which point I knew I had to tell him I didn't want to have kids.

Shayne was supportive and respectful and believed it was my decision. However, the key point here is that at no stage did I try to trick or deceive Shayne. I was always honest about my position when it came to children. I didn't want him to miss out on having them, if that is what he really wanted. I just knew it wasn't something I wanted.

There needs to be open and honest communication between you and your partner about what you truly want in life. Communication is key to your future happiness and to eliminate misunderstandings or uncertainty.

Similarly, Lyn Griffith, now fifty-two years old, remembers saying to her husband Rohan that he needed to be okay with her feelings about not wanting to have children. 'He was probably more keen to have kids in the earlier years, but I think that dwindled as we spent more time in kid-free environments.'

What I really hate is when women openly admit to tricking or intentionally failing pregnant to trap their partners into commitment. Some of the reasons women do this include: thinking he will love her more; because she really wants a child and will do anything to make that happen; to have a rich man's child; to get child support; to save a marriage; or to trick a man into marrying her. It's the old 'accidentally on purpose' trick.

This deception is really not cool, gals! How can any woman with a conscience live with herself after doing something so dishonest and deceptive with something that has such a massive impact on life? There should be lots of conversation around this very important topic before you commit to a life together.

Just some of the questions you'll want to talk about include:

- What happens if we cannot/do not fall pregnant?
- Can we support a child?
- What happens if the baby has a disability? Can we handle that?
- How will we split parenting duties?
- Who will be the main carer?
- Will we baptise them and what religion?
- Where are we raising them?
- What kind of delivery do we want?
- How strict are we going to be?
- What are the deal breakers for each of us?

These are all big questions that you should take the time to discuss with your partner. Tricking them into a major life decision will only lead to heartbreak, resentment and living a lie.

No one wants their child to be born with a dark spot in their memory of how he/she was conceived.

EVERYONE DESERVES THE RIGHT TO CHOOSE

Just like us chicks, men should be entitled to choose whether or not they want to be parents. Just look at George Clooney – self-confessed bachelor and first-time dad at age fifty-six. I guarantee no one was telling George he'd regret his decision!

Whether you want to have a child or not, you should be free to make that decision without pressure or judgement. And the same goes for the blokes.

I've always checked in with Shayne to ask if he is still happy with our decision, and he has always assured me he is. He is a great uncle and kids love him. He has a childlike quality and children just seem to gravitate towards him. I love that about him and at BBQs, he will often disappear, only to be found in the lounge room watching children's cartoons and movies with the kids. They love it and so does he.

However, he admits that keeping up with nieces, nephews and our friends' kids is more than enough for him. And he still gets to enjoy the freedom our childfree life gives us.

PART TWO

Making the right choice for you

'Honestly, we'd probably be great parents. But it's a human being, and unless you think you have excellent skills and have a drive or yearning in you to do that, the amount of work that that is and responsibility – I wouldn't want to screw them up! We love our animals.'

ELLEN DEGENERES

WHY DO YOU WANT WHAT YOU WANT?

With all of the noise around you, it can be hard to know what you really want. Do you want children, or is that just society/your up-bringing/your parents/your hormones talking? Do you want to be childfree, do you really want to rebel, or are there just some other things you want to do before you have kids?

In this part of the book, my goal is to help you make a choice that is authentic and true to yourself. While authenticity is the buzzword of the moment when it comes to marketing, I think it's a good word when it comes to the choice to have children or to be childfree. I want to be authentically me. I know who I am. I am more comfortable in a room of CEOs than changing nappies or watching kids in the playground.

A key piece of being authentic is understanding why you want what you want.

WHY WOMEN CHOOSE TO HAVE KIDS

Children that are born due to religion or obligation, to fix a failed marriage, or because of peer pressure or family expectation are born for the wrong reason. For some, becoming a mum is automatic, while, for others, it could be to feel accepted into an exclusive club on the other side. And, dare I say it, children are also born for a $3,000 baby bonus from the government.

There are, of course, many reasons why women choose to have children. Just a single generation ago, it was completely normal for a woman to graduate from high school, get married and have children.

Is it possible that women feel this pressure, instilled in them from a very young age, that they have to have children in order to feel fulfilled?

For some, parenthood is a hard-boiled belief; for others, it's a switch that flips after a crisis. Other times, it's just a feeling you get. Other reasons might include:

- To have someone to take care of you when you get old (which is not guaranteed)
- To carry on the family name
- Because you love babies
- It's human nature (for some)
- Pregnancy and child birth are life experiences
- To give your parents grandchildren
- To embody your love for each other
- You want your own bloodline

Hilary says, 'It has always been my number one ambition. I have always wanted to be a mum and create my own strong family unit.'

Catriona states, 'I didn't know if it was right for me. In fact, the thought of pregnancy, parenting and losing my lifestyle terrified me. I had been committed to children all my life through my work, but I also knew I would regret it if I never tried having one of my own.

You don't know what you don't know, and I am so glad I ended up doing it.'

Kim says, 'I've always known from a very young age that I wanted to be a parent and it's been really important to me. I've always gravitated towards nurturing and caring for others, and it makes me happy and content. I find kids delightful and I'm fascinated by how they develop. I didn't care if I gave birth to my own child or not. In fact, before we fell pregnant, we were looking into foster care and adoption, and will do so again. Biology doesn't really matter to me; I don't have a super strong urge to procreate as such – I just really want to be a mum.'

Linda says, 'I always wanted kids but my husband didn't. I was twenty-one when we met and I was okay with him not wanting kids and I focused on my career. Then in my thirties, I really knew I wanted kids. I fell pregnant at thirty-four and we just had our fourth baby. Now we can't picture what our lives were like before having kids.'

For many, having children has been a lifelong dream. For others, having kids seemed like a natural progression. And others didn't want to have children until they found the perfect partner, then they changed their mind. For others, however, having kids was an expectation. It's what their friends were doing, or they just always assumed or knew they would have kids.

Whatever the reason, you need to remember that being a parent is forever, so it's important to make the decision for the right reasons.

In my interviews with women on their decision to have children or be childfree, Tracey Mathers of Brisbane shared some wisdom her mother shared with her when she was younger: 'I always remember my mother saying to me, "Darling girl, think long and hard. Having a baby is more than buying pretty things and making them look gorgeous. You can't hand them back; you have them for life. Choose wisely." I think she may have known me better than anyone.'

WHY WOMEN CHOOSE NOT TO HAVE KIDS

During my research for this book and the many conversations I have had about this topic over the years, I've found that the reasons women choose to be childfree vary greatly. They might include fear, culture, past experience, bad childhood memories, lack of confidence, issues with a partner, choosing career over childbirth, financial circumstances, a lack of motivation or other priorities.

And I'm not the only one who's been researching this choice.

In a recent paper, sociologist Amy Blackstone of the University of Maine and Mahalia Dyer Stewart of UMass Amherst investigated the mechanics of the decision to be childfree. They found that childfree women were more outwardly focused in their decision-making, referencing how having kids would alter their adult relationships or contribute to overpopulation and other environmental impacts or that the world as it isn't hospitable to new children. They found that, at a macro level, the choice to have children is strongly correlated with education: The better educated people are, the fewer the children they have.

In a 2015 survey, The Huffington Post and YouGov surveyed 124 women on why they choose to be childfree. Their motivations ranged from preferring their current lifestyles to prioritising their careers, and the survey offered insight into the complex, layered decisions women make. Responses to the survey were varied and were classified under five broad categories: I want to prioritise my career; I don't like children; I have had a bad relationship; I don't want the financial responsibility; and I like my life as it is.

Even celebrities have been discussing their motivations for choosing to be childfree. In an interview with *Esquire* in August 2014, Cameron Diaz explained, 'It's so much more work to have children. To have lives besides your own that you are responsible for, I didn't take that on. That did make things easier for me. A baby, that's all day, every day for eighteen years. Not having a baby might really make things easier, but that doesn't make it an easy decision. I like protecting people, but I was never drawn to being a mother. I have it much easier than any of them. That's just what it is.'

Comedian Chelsea Handler has also been vocal about not wanting to have children, and recently interviewed Reece Witherspoon about the subject. Handler asked Witherspoon if she thought Handler was missing out by not having kids. Witherspoon was supportive of women who make that choice, saying, 'I really admire when women decide not to have kids because it is such a huge responsibility. If you in any way feel like you're not sure, then don't do it.'

According to IndexMundi, a site that compiles country data, there is a strong negative correlation between literacy and fertility rates worldwide. The countries with the highest literacy rates in the world, including places like Poland, Belarus, Estonia, Ukraine, Hungary, and others in central and Eastern Europe also have the world's lowest birth rates.

When I was doing research for this book, I also asked around. Here's what I found:

Nikki: 'I thought I wanted kids initially, however, after I got married, I just didn't want to share my husband with anybody! I felt like I'd waited so long for my "prince" to come along that I deserved to have him all to myself.

'But as the years have ticked by, I've had many other thoughts cross my mind. I lead a busy life, and I really enjoy quiet time; down time; relaxing time. If I had children, I would not get that. My husband and I can look to retire at a much younger age, having not had children. (Children are expensive!) We love holidays, and can go on beautiful holidays without children. I can think of nothing worse than raising a toddler in my forties, a tween/teenager in my fifties, and a young adult into my sixties. That thought is absolutely exhausting to me! I also hold grave fears for the state of the planet, and one of the biggest threats to the environment is over-population and consumerism. I get that some people may see some of those reasons as totally selfish and maybe they are. But they're honest.'

Lyn: 'I am basically selfish (that is not a criticism or condemnation of myself, but an observation). I like the good things in life, I like to be number one in my husband's life and I don't have a maternal bone in my body. Any day of the week I will cuddle a puppy or a kitten, but that's as far as it goes. If someone pushes a baby onto me, I am at a loss and out of my comfort zone. I don't feel comfortable with kids and, honestly, I really don't like them.'

Cate: 'I never had a maternal bone in my body – even when holding my nieces and nephews I'd worry about doing it wrong! I have always wanted to travel and live a life full of surprises and activities. I believe that and wanting to have a career would be the two major reasons for not having children. Also, of course, there is the lifelong impact – children stay at home longer these days, university expenses are higher and there is a lot more pressure on children with social media and the like.'

Michelle: 'Growing up, I always just assumed I would get married and have kids. There was probably no pressure as such to have kids, but it was always just a presumed thing, seeing that was what just happened in my family. I come from a family of three kids and both my brother and sister have five kids each. I have six cousins and they all have kids also so there was never really a doubt that I would have a family. However, I never fell pregnant after I got married and, after we divorced seven years later, children weren't an option financially.

'Now, at the age of forty-two, I am very happy with how my life is now without children. I really have lost all maternal feelings towards kids and now just get really clucky over puppy dogs instead. Travelling to as many places as possible is how I spend my money and time when I'm not working, and this to me is just perfect. Kids would not fit into this picture.'

Jae: 'I never ever wanted kids. I never ever wanted to get married either. I have always been incredibly ambitious; I established my own business in my early twenties and I loved working for myself. I loved the idea of building something; I loved having a huge, audacious goal.'

As for me, there are many reasons I don't want children.

I like my lifestyle as it is. I can sleep in (even though I'm usually up with the birds), travel, do what I want when I want, drink at 3pm, go shopping without bother, work until 8pm, go out every night, work on passion projects like this book... whatever I choose to. I choose freedom, experiences, travel and living every moment like I want to, full of possibilities.

I am not maternal. The thought of pregnancy and childbirth totally disgusts me. (Yes, I am one of those women who doesn't agree that it is beautiful! I cannot watch anything birth related, cannot look at pregnant women's stomachs and, no, I don't want to see any photos of your birth or watch you breastfeeding while I am eating my lunch.)

I never have been maternal with children and I'm not going to apologise for that. I will not get clucky when you bring your baby into the office, but I will swoon over a puppy. I remember clearly an incident in an office where someone came in with a newborn baby and everyone was milling around and getting all clucky. I was the one hiding at her desk, avoiding the 'oohs and ahhs' as much as possible. A few days later, though, I was head of the pack 'oohing and ahhing' over a little puppy. Being a mummy to puppies – tick! Being a mummy to little humans – no thank you!

Not every woman has that maternal gene. Not every woman wants to experience the wonders of pregnancy, change dirty diapers or do tuckshop duty. I choose to stay slim, have puppies, indulge in nice champagne, travel and buy beautiful shoes.

I am not shallow or selfish just because I do not want to be responsible for another person and how they turn out. I know what I was like when I got to high school – I don't know how my parents put up with me, let alone the financial commitment involved. Do I want to swap my Lexus and overseas holidays for a child? No, I don't. And I don't feel like I am missing out by spending my money on a trip to New York or a new pair of Jimmy Choo's instead of school fees and toys.

I love my freedom. I love being able to just jump in the car and go. We are a DINKS family (Double Income No Kids) and enjoy being able to head out for breakfast, run errands, go shopping, escape for the weekend, whatever it might be without the burden of baby bags and nappies. The times I have been with friends with either or babies or toddlers, it's been so hard. The time it takes to get ready to get out the door, then another ten minutes loading kids and gear into the car. No wonder they don't want to leave the house!

With 7.5 billion people on earth, overpopulation is one of the biggest problems we're currently facing. Overpopulation contributes to global warming, pollution, extinction and the consumption of natural resources. Children have a significant carbon footprint, so by not having them I am doing my bit to stay green and help the planet for the next generation.

Another factor is the number of unwanted children already in society. In the US, there are 45,000 children in foster care at any one time. The impacts of this on society are massive. And what of children in third-world countries who need to be saved from famine and war? With so many children out there who need love and support already, why add one more?

I am OCD organised. I don't like delays of any kind messing with my schedule. If I scheduled one hour to run errands, that's what I've got. I know it's crazy, but I need to keep control of my time to fit everything in. My brain barely stops. Even when I say to myself I'm going to watch a movie or chill by the pool, I don't go long before I'm typing notes into my phone. (Literally, these words are being typed into my iPhone while I'm sitting by the pool relaxing in Cairns. I can't help myself.)

I cannot even imagine trying to fit kids into my crazy scheduled life. I really don't know how that could possibly work. I hear people say that if you have kids, you just make it work for you, but I don't want to. I have watched as friends have done the juggling act and while they choose to do it, I have designed my life to my ideal specifications and there is no room for a child in that equation.

And I don't believe in having kids for the sake of having kids. While I have seen many children born out of love, I have seen too many children brought into this world for the wrong reasons. Too many who are used as bargaining tools in failing relationships or who are born out of obligation, not desire. Too many created for financial gain (thank the Australian Government for those ones) and too many who are treated poorly and abused.

But that's just me. The real question is: What do *you* want?

WHAT'S YOUR 'WHY'?

In an earlier chapter, I mentioned psychologist Talya Rabinovitz, who works with women in their thirties and forties who don't want children but have anxiety around their choice. She says, 'It can be hard to separate your true self and what you really want from your conditioned self – that of what society says you should want. I think it's important to consider how your life might look if you don't follow the standard social script of being a woman.'

There are also a lot of comparisons between women, which makes things more difficult. We live in a voyeuristic world, as Facebook and other social platforms act as windows into our lives. We have unprecedented access to the lives of our friends, family and acquaintances and vice versa.

It's easy to get lost in comparisons, or start fearing you've made the wrong decision, especially when looking at how happy everyone looks in their family or holiday snaps.

Don't get caught up in the comparison game. This book is not about comparing lives. It is about showing the lives that come of the different choices we make and supporting and celebrating each other for the choices we make.

So, how do you stop getting lost in everyone else's expectations, and reconnect with what you want?

An exercise you might try is to list out is the good old pros and cons. As crazy as that sounds, it is a great exercise to help you view the practicality and emotion behind having a child. Just start writing and make the lists as long as you want.

Simply:

1. Divide a piece of paper into two columns.

2. In the first column, list the pros of having kids – the reasons why you might like to have them. Is it something you've always wanted? Do you love playing with young children or helping them with their homework? Do you like the idea of teaching someone how to be a good person? Write down whatever is true for you.

3. In the second column, list the cons, or the reasons why you don't think you'd like to have them. This might include the financial responsibility, the loss of freedom, the negative aspects of kids (diaper changes, temper tantrums and so on), uncertainty about whether or not your partner wants them (if you have a partner), concerns about your age and more. Again, write down what's true for you.

4. Once you're comfortable that you've gotten everything out, review each of your lists and note which of the reasons are most important to you. For example, if you really want kids, you might feel an overwhelming surge of joy at the thought of holding your own baby in your arms – that feeling is probably going to outweigh the annoyance of changing the baby's nappy. On the other hand, if you get that feeling of joy from buying a new pair of shoes or travelling to an exotic destination, that would outweigh having kids for reasons that focus on obligation or social pressure.

5. Rewrite your lists with just the things that are most important to you.

As you're doing this exercise, know that there are no right or wrong answers. Additionally, this should be from your perspective only and should not include what other people might think or want. Remember, you're determining *your* 'whys'.

Also keep in mind that just because you have a bigger list on one side, it doesn't mean you will choose that option. This is one of the reasons why I recommend going through the list a second time and figuring out what's really important to you, as these should be the pieces that guide you, rather than what you think you 'should' be writing down, or others' expectations.

Once you've been through this exercise, you should have a better idea of what you really want.

One of the exercises Tayla does with her clients is to separate between society's expectations and their personal values. She says, 'We separate what is really important to them personally from the things they are told they should care about by society.'

Many of us don't know our values. We don't understand what's most important to us. Instead, we focus on what our society, culture and media value. To help you define your personal values, here are some steps to determine what they are:

- Ensure you adopt a positive mindset and open your mind doing this exercise.

- Grab a sheet of paper and find a comfortable place to sit.

- Now, consider various experiences in your life. Meaningful moments, happy times, positive experiences, and make a note of them. What values were you honouring during those times?

- Next, consider negative moments and experiences – what made you angry, frustrated, resentful? What value was being suppressed?

- Finally, consider what is most important in your life. Is it health, creativity, adventure, beauty, etc.? What are the personal values you must honour for you to feel good about yourself?

- Combine all these answers to create a master list of personal values.

- You will likely have a lot, so the next step is to group these values under related themes. E.g. values like learning, growth and development relate to each other. Connection, belonging and intimacy are related, too. Group them together and select a word that best describes that group.

- To further narrow down the list, consider what values are essential in your life.
- Finally, rank them in order of importance. You may need to do this step in multiple sittings. After doing one round of ranking, put it aside and sleep on it.
  - A few days later, go back and review your list. How do they make you feel? Do you feel they are consistent with who you are? Are they personal to you?

So, if you are unsure, take some time to define what your personal values are. Don't worry about the values you get told you should care about; list the values that you personally hold. This is a great exercise to help you understand yourself better.

IT'S TIME TO DO WHAT YOU WANT

More women need to stand behind what they truly want and not give in to peer pressure and expectation. You can be happy with children, and you can be happy being childfree. What you don't want is to make a choice only to regret it later (more on this shortly).

Talking to women of all ages soon reveals a wide range of reasons for having children. Some say they wanted a baby from when they were kids themselves. For many, the desire is not very strong as a young adult but increases in their thirties and forties. And some are just not interested. For many of the women who have children later, it's not that they have put off something they have wanted for a long time or that they are having a child just because the baby shop is closing – the urge to have a child is just not there earlier. Everyone is different and, therefore, everyone should make their own rules.

You can be confident and happy about being childfree, just as you can be confident and happy about being a mum. The difference is that you just derive your sense of fulfilment from different areas of life.

Choosing not to have children is as valid as choosing to have them, so make sure you choose for you.

'I didn't want to – and I'm glad I don't – have any children. God only knows what I would have done with them, poor things. I really do like kids, but there wouldn't have been room in my life to raise children. I was so involved with my career and I would have had to give up the career in large part because I could not possibly have short changed the child.'

LILY TOMLIN

THE MANY ROADS TO FULFILMENT

In society, there's an assumption that 'family' includes children, and that **not** having kids must be the result of infertility. It's an accident, not a choice.

These attitudes are at odds with changes in the way people are living. From the 1970s to the 2000s, the number of childless women in the US nearly doubled, and national data suggests that fifteen per cent of women and twenty-four per cent of men will hit the age of forty without having kids.

So, what do their lives look like instead? As I mentioned last chapter, fulfilment comes in many forms, and you don't need to become a mother in order to be fulfilled (unless it's genuinely important to you, of course). In this chapter, I'll share some of the other forms of fulfilment that childfree women enjoy.

PUPPIES OVER PARENTHOOD

There are increasing numbers of people adopting pets rather than having kids, with the Oxford Dictionary adding the term 'fur baby' to its official lexicon in 2015.

In its 2016 comprehensive survey of Australian pet owners, Animal Medicines Australia, the peak body representing manufacturers of veterinary medicines, found increasing numbers of people (sixty-four per cent, up from fifty-nine per cent in 2013) regard their dog as a member of the family rather than just a companion (twenty-three per cent). (I include myself in the former.)

An AMA report shows that Australians spent more than $12 billion on pets and pet products in 2016. Nearly forty-four per cent of pet owners said their pet substituted for having a partner or children. And about sixty per cent said owning a pet was less stressful than having children.

The trend is not just in Australia. In the US, data from the Center for Disease Control and Prevention shows that a big drop in the number of babies born to women from age fifteen to twenty-nine corresponds with a huge increase in the number of tiny pooches owned by young US women. There is even talk of naming the next generation of youngsters 'Generation Rex', with playgrounds around New York city being quiet while dog runs are packed.

Dog-crazy New York ladies told *The Post* that they aren't surprised by the findings – and that they happily gave up diaper changes, temper tantrums and college funds for the easy affection of their doggy 'child'.

Meanwhile, as Japan's birth rate plummets, the estimated worth of its pet industry has risen to $10 billion, with pampered pooches enjoying holidays at hot spring resorts, yoga classes and designer clothes. The country has twenty-two million pets, compared to just seventeen million children under the age of fifteen.

In a smart and expensive neighbourhood of Tokyo, eye surgeon Toshiko Horikoshi has a private clinic, a stylish apartment, a grand piano, a Porsche and two pet pooches: Tinkerbell, a Chihuahua, and

Ginger, a poodle. 'Japanese dog owners think a dog is like a child,' says Horikoshi. 'I have no children, so I really love my two dogs.'

Many women with dogs are spending crazy amounts of money on designer dog clothes, pet jewellery and even tiny shoes. Horikoshi says she shops for her dogs most weekends and they get new clothes each season. In many parts of Tokyo, it is easier to buy clothes for dogs than for children. Boutiques sell everything from frilly frocks to designer jeans, from nappies to organic nibbles, and smart 'doggie bags' and buggies or pushchairs to transport them in.

Three in ten British couples choose to raise a dog rather than a child. It seems they are putting off parenthood and choosing to get a pet instead and the most popular 'fur kid' is a dog, which is no surprise to me.

A study of 2,000 Brits was commissioned by animal charity the Blue Cross to highlight the role that pets play in our lives, coining the term 'generation pet' to describe the trend for choosing pets over children. The research also reveals that sixty-one per cent of Brits believe that getting a dog before having children puts you into the right mindset for becoming a parent.

Some forwarded-thinking businesses in the UK are also giving animal-mad employees time off when they get a new pet. Yes, paw-ternity leave is a new thing. Almost one in twenty new pet owners in the UK has been offered paw-ternity leave by their employers, according to new research by pet insurance provider Petplan.

Just like standard parental leave for new mums and dads, employees are granted the time off in addition to their standard holiday allowance. One of the first companies to introduce the policy was

Mars Petcare, which has sites across the UK and manufactures many leading pet foods, including Whiskas and Pedigree Chum. Some firms allow workers to take a few hours off to settle in a new household animal, while others offer as much as several weeks paid time off. The leave can be used to carry out training, attend vet appointments or simply spend more time with a new animal. The company's HR director, Kate Menzies, said: 'We know how important it is to take an animal into your home, and we want to enable and ease responsible pet ownership for our employees.'

The first company in the United States to offer paw-ternity benefits is beer maker BrewDog, a Scottish brewery that opened an Ohio location in 2017. They now offer a week of paid leave for employees with new puppies or rescued dogs. BrewDog said the benefit will be offered to all of its nearly 1,000 employees across the world.

Although the Ministry of Business, Innovation and Employment in the USA said it did not know how many companies were currently offering pet leave, Aidan Burch, its acting manager of employment standards, said it encouraged firms to think of unique ways to attract staff.

HarperCollins India is also offering paw-ternity leave. The tail-wagging perk, put into effect in 2017, grants five working days of paid leave for staffers who have just adopted a pet. This gives them a week to bond and to help the fur babies adjust to their new homes, which anyone who's ever struggled with a crying puppy or kitten that pees all over the house can appreciate.

The publishing house will also let workers bring their pets into designated animal-friendly areas in the office. It's part of keeping workers happy and also encouraging responsible pet adoption.

Unfortunately, paw-ternity leave doesn't yet exist in Australia. However, almost forty per cent of Australian animal owners took time off work when they got a new pet, a PETstock Pet Parent Survey has revealed, while a further forty-three per cent would consider doing so. More than half of people took one to three carers days off work, but an astonishing one in five clocked off for up to a week.

So, why fur kids? What's sparking the trend?

Research shows that looking at a dog can give you the same rush of emotion as looking at a baby thanks to oxytocin, or the 'love' hormone. This hormone is released while breast-feeding and during loving physical contact. Scientists at Azabu University in Japan have recently discovered that dog owners experience a rush of this feel-good hormone when they interact with their dogs – just like the mothers of new babies.

According to Psychology Today, pet owners have better self-esteem, fitness, sociability and happiness than non-pet-owners. They also have lower blood pressure and cholesterol.

Cost is also a factor. While the cost of having a child varies from person to person, the most recent of a series of studies from the National Centre for Social and Economic Modelling estimated that the typical middle-income Australian family spends $812,000 raising two children from birth to twenty-one years. This equates to $19,300 per child per year, roughly in line with international estimates from other high-income countries.

Personally, I have always chosen puppies over parenthood. My three fur babies – Tia, Latte and Neo – were all fostered and then adopted from the RSPCA. We are classified as failed foster parents – a term I can happily live with knowing that I have given a furever home to my three dogs.

My dogs have been taught to sit, shake and stay. They are not allowed to run uncontrolled in any environment and, as pet parents, we are always conscious of making sure they don't annoy other people.

My dogs love me unconditionally, they never answer back, and they don't ask for money or for me to drop them at a friend's house to play on Saturday night when I want to relax with a few wines. My dogs allow me so much more freedom than a child could. Dogs are also cheaper and fit in with my lifestyle. I don't have to decline invitations because its puppy nap time, and they are happy to sit and watch a movie of my choice with me. And my dogs are better behaved than many kids I see racing around shopping centres and screaming on planes.

Just because I am not a mum doesn't mean I cannot be maternal. I feel maternal about my fur kids and want to love and protect them, just like people do with human kids.

Does it matter where your love comes from? Dog or child? Love is love! So, find the love that's right for you.

BEING A ROCKSTAR AUNTY

There are also plenty of childfree women who have oodles of love, affection and advice to share with nieces, nephews and friends' kids as their honorary aunties.

Non-mothers' roles as advocates, mentors and friends to children are well documented. The founder of Savvy Auntie Melanie Notkin's

'Shades of Otherhood' survey shows that eighty per cent of non-moms aged twenty to forty-four play an active role in a child's life. The survey also found that eighty per cent of non-mums felt they could lead a happy life without children, whether or not they want children of their own.

Another study, 'Digital Women Influences Study – The power of PANK', found that it's common for aunts to spend money on the children in their lives and assist kids' parents financially. In fact, in 2012, aunts spent an estimated $387 on each child in their lives.

In recognition of the importance of these women, Melanie Notkin started a national day to celebrate childfree women who are loving aunts or godmothers. The ninth annual Aunties Day was held on the twenty-third of July, 2017, to celebrate and honour aunts by relation, aunts by choice to friends› children, godmothers, and all women who play an active role in the life of a child not-their-own.

An aunt is there to provide 'QualAuntie Time' and experiences as a loving caregiver and 'ConfidAunt' to her nieces and nephews from the day they are born and as they grow up. Many women without children of their own also give tirelessly to children all over the world. These 'BenevolAunts' are due their day to be honoured.

Elizabeth Gilbert says it well in her May 2014 blog: 'I have come to believe there are three sorts of women, when it comes to questions of maternity. There are women who are born to be mothers, women who are born to be aunties, and women who should not be allowed within ten feet of a child. It's really important to know which category you belong to. Now, listen, if you put a baby in front of me, rest assured: that baby is going to get cuddled, spoiled and adored. But even as I'm loving on that beautiful infant, I know in my heart: This is not my destiny. It never was. And there is a curious rush of joy that I feel, knowing this to be true, for it is every bit as important in life to understand who you are not, as to understand who you are. Me, I'm just not a mum. Having reached a contented and productive middle age, I can say without a blink of hesitation that I wouldn't trade my choices for anything.'

For me, I love being an aunty and godmother. There is nothing better than visiting my nieces and nephews, spoiling them and then going home to enjoy a quiet night watching a movie with some wine and peace and quiet.

I consider myself a PANK – Professional Aunty, No Kids. The way I see it, I get the best of both worlds. I get to experience the fun side of kids and then, when I've had enough, I can retreat to the little haven that I call home.

As an aunty, I get to be a role model. I want my nieces, Hannah and Caitlin, to see that they do have a choice as a strong, independent woman to follow their dreams and desires. I want them to see that they can make a choice that is not traditional and that won't always be popular with others. Even though they are both being raised in a very traditional home, I want them to know they have choices. I will support them, no matter what choices they make, but I hope that they do not feel pressure or expectation to do things that maybe they don't want to, simply due to what they have been exposed to.

I want them to be able to come to me with their problems, so I can help guide them based on my experiences in life. I know that, when

I was growing up, I often found it easier to talk to someone other than my parents.

I think as aunties we offer a different perspective to kids than their parents can. Our guidance is less biased, because we usually aren't as invested in certain futures for these kids. And, even though it still comes from love, we have the emotional distance that enables a different type of dialogue.

I think the effort we make with our nieces and nephews (and our adopted ones) is appreciated. We make sure we celebrate the big birthdays with something special, including some one-on-one time with us. We will always be there to support them throughout their lives and chosen careers. My husband Shayne is an avid rugby league fan and our godson, Daniel, is a promising sixteen-year-old football star. Shayne flies down to Newcastle to watch him play at least one game each season. (Though I think he's also living a little vicariously through Daniel, too. Unfulfilled footy dreams and all that...)

My sister says that as an aunty I am very important to her children. 'They get so excited to see you and love spending time with their aunty Tan. And, as a mum, I think it's nice they have someone else to talk to and look up to.'

As you might have realised, I do not hate children. I just don't want to be a parent. I love their energy and innocence and the way they see the world. Sometimes, I wish I was a kid again and had their childish views. Wasn't life so much easier back then?

However, I have never changed a nappy, fed a baby, bathed a baby or pushed a pram (apart from when I was a little girl) and I don't have any desire to do so. None of that is appealing in the least. I am proud of the fact that I haven't done any of those things.

I give kids cuddles, buy them treats, encourage their creativity, colour in with them, take them on outings for special occasions and give them advice. Being a rockstar aunty is an important job, after all!

There are multiple paths to motherhood and multiple ways to act as a mothering influence with children. It is my mission to be the best rockstar aunty I can be. Not everyone was supposed to be a mum, and I one of those chosen few.

CAREER & BUSINESS

For me, career and business has always been a big focus in my life.

In the workplace, people all too often assume women with no children must be putting their careers ahead of having kids. While true for some, this is not true for all. I don't want to generalise this section, as not all childfree women are 'career crazy', as they can be labelled. While I am one of those ambitious and driven career women, being able to focus on career, for me, was a by-product or side effect of not having children, not the sole reason for not having them.

Career and business is another road to fulfilment for many childfree women, but not the only one. For me, I have always defined myself by my career and the work I do.

Being childfree has allowed me to spend more time on education, improving my personal skills, networking and travelling for work. Not having to consider or worry about scheduling time for school pickups, after school activities, sickness or the like means I have total and 100 per cent control of how my working life has been spent. Not having to consider anyone else in my decision-making does make a big difference.

It has allowed me to move around the country, often on short notice, as my dear husband can attest to. I remember in my late twenties telling my husband that I wanted to move to QLD and his response was, 'Get a job first, then we can move.' So, I did! However, he was thinking South East QLD and my new role was in Cairns. We had four weeks to pack up our house, find somewhere to live and travel to Cairns. It was just us and our three fur babies and we have not looked back. This has happened several times and would have been made much harder, if not impossible, to do in a few short weeks if I had had children.

Raising a child is time-consuming. Childfree women have additional time to devote to their careers. They value the time and effort it takes to become secure in a career and they are enjoying the intellectual and monetary perks it provides. Choosing other pathways to personal satisfaction, it seems, can be equally and, for some, more gratifying than being a mother.

In a **Psychology Today** article, 'Choosing to be Childfree in a Changing World', author Ellen Walker states that forty-three per cent of college-educated women between the ages of thirty-three and forty-six are child-free.

And according to a National Bureau of Economic Research study, choosing to have kids can hurt women's chances for advancement and lower their earning potential. Having a child *costs the average high-skilled woman $230,000* in lost lifetime wages relative to similar women who never gave birth.

The US Pew Research Center's 2015 *Women and Leadership* study asked respondents when women with leadership aspirations should have children. While thirty-six per cent of people said it should happen early in her career, forty per cent said later in the career, and twenty-two per cent said that the best choice would be not to have children.

Many childfree women think having children would be a distraction they don't want or need as they focus on their career, knowing there is a clear path for them.

However, some women, like Kelda Rheinberger, manage to enjoy both children and a successful career. 'I am not really sure I decided I didn't want to have children, though I did know I did not want to make a decision until later in life. In my late twenties, I was faced with the possibility that I may not be able to have children. As fate would have it, I fell pregnant the following year and felt that it was meant to be. Hard to explain and may seem a little crazy, but it really felt right, like it was meant to be. When I found out I was pregnant, I recall feeling quite overwhelmed with feelings of excitement, though at the same time I was quite daunted at the thought of being both pregnant and a mother and whether or not I was maternal enough. Though, somehow, these feelings seemed to intrinsically dissolve – not sure how or why, they just did. I also had a very strong maternal urge to have more children and if I did not or could not, somehow my life would not have been complete and I would have felt like something was missing.'

Kelda has had a very successful corporate career while being a wife and mother to three children, so it is possible to have both.

I know, for me, my career is massively rewarding and it has allowed me to embark on personal business pursuits while working full time. In 2006, I started an online shoe store while I was working in a corporate job. Shoes were (and still are) a passion of mine and I funded that business with my commissions from that role. Not having kids made it possible to dedicate myself to my career and building a business on the side. I had the time and resources to be able to do both. And when you love what you do, it doesn't feel like work. It is just an extension of my life and how I spend my time.

Nearly four years ago, after leaving a previous corporate role, I started my current business, Digital Conversations (www.digitalconversations.com.au) – so, get in touch if you're in the market for some digital help! (Hey, I had to get in some self-promotion #marketer). As much as running a business can be a total rollercoaster ride (much like life), I am not sure how I would've managed the long hours, stress, networking, anxiety and everything it entails if I had had children. I know there are many 'mumpreneurs' out there doing exactly that and I salute them for being able to balance both, however, it is not for me. I want 100 per cent focus on business, without distraction. That is a choice myself and other childfree women make to suit our life. And there is nothing wrong with that.

Regardless of what your choices are, for childfree women, the freedom to just pick up and go makes climbing the career ladder an option that might not be as readily available to mums.

TRAVEL, EXPERIENCES, FREEDOM

I love travelling, I love being free, and so I keep leaving the sun and the sea but my heart lies waiting over the foam... Hang on, I might have borrowed those lines from a classic aussie song (insert cheeky smile here).

We have travelled the world and will continue to do so for the rest of our lives. Our first overseas trip together was to Bali when I was twenty, and we are always planning our next big and small adventures.

We've gambled in Vegas, had a private dinner on Hayman island, shopped (a lot) in New York, rowed a boat in Central Park, had my photo taken with Mickey Mouse at Disneyland, shopped the markets in Hong Kong, gotten cheap massages in China, mixed with the dead in the Tower of London, been star spotting in LA, had a private island tour around Vanuatu, haggled in Bali, swum in the crystal clear waters of the Caribbean, danced in Miami, enjoyed the view from the top of the Eiffel Tower, ridden gondolas in Venice, partied in Mykonos and so many other experiences in between. These are memories I treasure and, to me, they are priceless.

Travel, for me, is not to escape life, but experience it. Travelling opens up a whole new world of experiences and offers perspective on what a tiny place we as individuals occupy in the world. I cannot imagine not travelling and struggle to understand why anyone would not want to see other parts of the world.

I love experiencing new things and I am always looking for places locally and far far away that we can go and experience. Being childfree makes it easy for me to have many new experiences every year (#yolo).

The freedom to be able to just go is like no other. We can call the pet sitter if it is an extended stay or just head out on the town if we feel like it. It is much easier getting a pet sitter than a baby sitter with short notice.

As much as travelling without kids is amazing, unfortunately, much of the time, we aren't actually travelling without kids so much as we are travelling with other people's kids, an experience which can be extremely frustrating and stressful.

I have had many bad experiences on planes, from kids kicking the back of my seat on long haul flights to screaming babies to mothers letting their kids yell and generally misbehave appallingly, with no consideration for anyone else on the plane.

We recently stayed at a beautiful resort in Kingscliff for several nights and there was one family whom I am certain the entire resort would've been glad to see check out. There were other children also staying but these two children were literally screaming and running havoc in the pool area (I could even hear them in another part of the resort while having a massage). I was dumbfounded as the parents did little to stop their behaviour and I watched couple after couple leave the pool. It was the one thing that ruined a close to perfect experience.

In general, when you ask to be moved or for the staff to do something about it, you are made to feel bad, and that is very wrong. Why is my experience and comfort any less important than a mother's?

Just because you choose to travel with your kids, it doesn't mean I have to, and I am a big advocate of childfree travel options. Give me a childfree haven any day where my serenity is not shattered by the ear-piercing cries from OPBs (Other People's Babies).

On a Caribbean cruise we took several years ago, there was an Adults Only section at the top of the ship, where I spent much of my time. These are becoming very popular in resorts and on cruise ships. There are no longer entirely childfree resorts and childfree restaurants, but childfree flights seem to be taking off (pun intended).

In 2012, Malaysia Airlines announced that they would provide a childfree seating area on one of their flights. A Trip Advisor survey found forty-two per cent of respondents would pay to sit in a childfree section. Another poll out of the United Kingdom revealed that over fifty per cent of adults advocate for childfree flights, and almost two-thirds of those surveyed indicated that loud children are the biggest in-flight annoyance, bypassing bad food and limited space. C'mon Virgin and Qantas, when are you going to catch up and provide a childfree zone?

On April 1st 2012, WestJet announced their new program, 'Kargo Kids', in which children would be put in the cargo area of the plane, provided with toys and a trough-feed, and allowed to run and play freely, thus providing a serene ambience for adults on board. Of course, it was an April Fool's Day joke, but what a hilarious image!

Another big reason for not having kids is freedom. The definition of freedom is the power or right to act, speak or think as one wants. Bring it on! I cannot even imagine having everything I do being dictated by a child. Freedom allows me to put myself first. That is not selfish; that is simply me living my life for me and not someone else.

The word childfree says it all – free! Free to do whatever we want to do in a day. Yes, we still have responsibilities, but our freedom gives us more choices and fewer limitations. Our obligations are very different to those of parents.

I came across this quote which I think adds an interesting perspective: 'There are other things that could give the same happiness without the resultant misery that having kids brings. Like a significant other. I'd rather hear the person I chose to spend my life with say "I love you" than someone who drains me of energy and depends on me for everything and never gives me a second to myself.'

But that's just my choice.

HOW CHILDFREE WOMEN GIVE BACK

As childfree women, there are a lot of ways that we give back to society, too.

Contrary to stereotypes, childfree adults find plenty to do besides hoard wealth and travel the world. A piece published in *The Economist* in July 2017 looked at how adults without children give back to society in the absence of raising a child. It cites a German study that found that forty-two per cent of charitable foundations are started by childless people, who make up roughly eleven per cent of the worldwide adult population. Along the same lines, forty-eight per cent of married, childless adults aged fifty-five and older have set up wills entrusting some money to charities. For parents, the number drops to twelve per cent.

Benefits of giving include a feeling of fulfilment, knowing you have helped someone less fortunate, you have made a positive impact, and you are providing for someone that truly needs the support and help. We are helping improve economies and we support causes and charities that make the world a better place to live.

Plus, studies have found health benefits associated with giving and helping others. According to a study published in the International Journal of Psychophysiology, people who gave social support to others had lower blood pressure and stress levels, increased self esteem, less depression and greater happiness than people who didn't.

We all have causes that resonate with our core beliefs. For me, I gravitate towards causes that help women in business, that help girls get access to educate and that provide help for animals who have no voice. I do a lot of charitable giving to many other causes, however, these are ones that have always personally resonated with me.

From the age of five to sixteen, I sponsored a young girl in Ghana through World Vision. I got a lot of satisfaction knowing I was helping to provide education and a better quality of life for a girl who might never be lucky enough to have the same opportunities as me. Although I didn't get to meet her, I did get regular letters and drawings, and I would like to think that my support impacted greatly on her life, even though it was a relatively small amount that came out of my pocket each month.

I also love the work that One Girl does to educate girls in third world countries. This is a cause that not only resonates with me, but allows me to provide in another way for children who actually need my help. These are girls with no access to traditional education. For them, education is based on wealth and, often, these girls are forced to go to work to help their families rather than to school to learn and build a future. They don't have a choice and I believe that education should be a right for every girl on this earth.

Education provides knowledge, which gives these girls choices to consider in their lives. This is something that they have not previously had. That is powerful and it means they are able to change their lives and their families' lives.

I have also supported many women through Kiva, which provides microloans to people all over the world. These microloans help people outside of traditional banks who wouldn't otherwise get a chance to get a loan. It provides them with the help and step up they need to make a real difference to their lives and their children's lives. The reasons they need the loans are many and include: funding small businesses, paying for education, growing crops for their community, helping with medical expenses and building homes. I have loaned several thousand dollars over the past few years and always reinvest this back into more Kiva loans. I get a big warm and fuzzy feeling knowing I am providing real help directly where it is needed.

Through giving back, childfree people can use their greater freedom to advocate for causes that parents often don't have the time to carry the baton on. I don't believe I would have been able to give back the way I do today if I'd had children, as my priorities would be different. In this way, I love how we complement each other!

Childfree adults don't just pay it forward through advocacy and charitable contributions. Not having children is one of the most effective choices a person can make to fight climate change and the mass extinction of nonhuman species. It's certainly the single most impactful way to reduce one's carbon footprint.

Having children is the most destructive thing a person can to do to the environment, according to a study from researchers from Lund University in Sweden. They found having one fewer child per family can save 'an average of 58.6 tonnes of CO2-equivalent emissions per year'.

In industrialized countries, one person could save 2.4 metric tons of CO2 a year living car-free, 1.6 from avoiding a single trans-Atlantic flight and 0.8 by changing to a vegetarian diet, researchers have found. But having one fewer child blows those figures out of the water, with a reduction of more than fifty-eight tons of carbon emissions per year. Hey, the numbers don't lie!

FIND WHAT FULFILS YOU

As women, we are all different and that is a great thing. Geez, if everyone were the same as me, I'd struggle (as would hubby, who tells me one of me is enough).

As we navigate this thing called life, we need to work out what it is that fulfils us and allows us to be who we want to be. Both having and foregoing children come with benefits and costs. While the moral good of having children has never been in doubt, today there is real value in not having children, too.

In an episode of Sex and the City, Sam asks Carrie what her life would look like if she never had a baby. Carrie responds with, 'Him, sex, travel, comfort, love and extraordinary adventures.' Not too shabby! These are fulfilling and acceptable life choices, just like having a child. For me, I love being childfree and feel very happy and fulfilled

There are many paths to fulfilment. They all look different but, in the end, you can get to the same destination – happiness and living the life you choose for you.

So, the real question is: What lights you up? What are the things you are passionate about and that make you smile?

Whether you have children, are childfree or are childless, you can find the path that is most fulfilling for you.

'I'm completely happy not having children. I mean, everybody does not have to live in the same way. And as somebody said, "Everybody with a womb doesn't have to have a child any more than everybody with vocal cords has to be an opera singer."'

GLORIA STEINEM

LIVE IN A REGRET-FREE ZONE

We've covered a lot of terrain in this book, discussing the social and cultural influences that push us to become mothers, the pressure from friends and family and the judgement from other women, the relationship between motherhood and identity, and the myth of the biological clock. One of the things I've learnt while exploring this topic is how many women make the decision to have children (or even to be childfree) for the wrong reasons.

Ultimately, motherhood is put on a pedestal as the Holy Grail. What this means is that while some women genuinely want to have kids, many feel pressured into making a decision that they'll later regret.

Having children for these reasons is almost like a type of FOMO syndrome. The fear of missing out on something that you want or think you might want.

Everyone is afraid of something. For me, it was living a life I didn't want or choose. I could not do that. I was always told I could do, be and have anything I wanted in life. And the life I wanted did not include children.

For many women, that fear could be around failure: What if I don't have kids – does that make me a failure as a woman? Fear of judgement: What will other women or my family think of me? Fear of the unknown: What impact will this decision have on my life? What will my life look like with or without kids?

What if? What if? What if?

You don't want to live your life wondering 'what if?' The key to this is making a decision that's true for you. Never live your life to make other people happy. At the end of the day, you are the only one that has to walk in your shoes!

THE IMPORTANCE OF BEING TRUE TO YOURSELF

In the book *The Top Five Regrets of the Dying,* Bronnie Ware shares that the top regret people have on their deathbeds is wishing they'd had the courage to be true to themselves, not the lives others expected of them.

The other regrets people have are that they wish they hadn't worked so hard, had the courage to express their feelings, had stayed in touch with friends and had let themselves be happier.

Being true to yourself always exists at the core of who you are. When you are being true to yourself, you are completely honest about what you feel, deeply value and desire. It also means communicating your feelings wholeheartedly both to yourself and others, allowing your truth to flow through you and into the world.

You don't have to fit in or be like everyone else. You may start to become someone others want you to be instead of who you truly are, without even realising it. Eventually, this may lead to frustration and you may not even know why this is so.

You are unique for a reason. Don't deny what makes you happy.

Having a child when it isn't something you truly want is something you could regret for years to come.

According to a study conducted by the US Department of Health and Human Services between 2002 and 2003, of the more than 7,000 mothers surveyed, an overwhelming ninety-seven per cent believe the rewards of being a parent outweigh the cost. But what about the three per cent of mothers who disagree?

'Saying you regret having your kids just seems so profoundly norm-violating,' says Robin Simon, a Wake Forest College sociology professor who specialises in the mental health effects of parenting. 'I don›t think that very many parents do regret it, in part because the ideology is so powerful. They don›t regret it, they›re just like, "Wow, I didn›t know it would be this hard."'

Orna Donath, an Israeli sociologist specialising in gender and women›s health at Ben-Gurion University of the Negev, is one of the few academics to tackle the subject. Last year, she conducted interviews with a group of twenty-three mothers, including five grandmothers, who all said they regretted giving birth. She determined regret by asking two key questions: 'If you could go back, with the knowledge and experience you have now, would you still become a mother?' and 'From your point of view, are there advantages to motherhood?' All of the mothers in the study answered the first question negatively, and if they answered yes to the second question, they were asked a third: 'From your point of view, do the advantages outweigh disadvantages?' They all responded with a resounding no.

There is even a Facebook group that was founded in 2012 for parents who regret having children, which shows there are plenty of women out there who feel this way.

When Isabella Dutton wrote about regretting motherhood for *The Daily Mail* in 2013, she received a storm of criticism online. The most 'liked' comment on the article called her 'an utterly miserable, cold-hearted and selfish woman'.

Backlash aside, the article also resonated with parents who identified with Dutton›s regret and admired her honesty.

It's no wonder, however, that more women don't speak honestly about the challenges of being a mother. This type of bullying, judgement and unwarranted and unwelcome criticism does not allow for a solid and honest conversation around the challenges, which is unfair and wrong.

It also leads to more women deciding to have children for the wrong reasons, or without realising how hard it can be.

It's essential to be true to yourself in all aspects of life, but especially when it comes to the choice of whether or not to have children.

As Ware says, 'We are taught that if you decide to do something for yourself you are selfish. However, learning to express your own needs, clearly and unapologetically, is the first step towards living a happier life. Understand the difference between should and want as one is a choice, the other duty.

'It takes courage to ask ourselves difficult questions and to take a good look at our fears and what we have become. But in the end, it can lead us to be more courageous, more present, more connected to our lives and the people we share it with. We have to decide if the pain of remaining exactly where we are is worth more than the pain of change. Standing true to your beliefs can be lonely at times but you are true to your calling when you live with the courage to be yourself.'

Whose life are you living? Do you live to please others at the expense of living a life that reflects your values? Is your life directed by the expectations of others or by chance?

When you look back on your life, have you lived a life true to you? Or have you lived a life someone else wanted? Be honest here, because as long as you are happy with your choices and you're being authentically you, then I'm happy for you. But if you aren't, then what are you afraid of?

These are big questions to ask but they are important, as having a child is one choice you cannot undo.

Regardless of your choice, we have an opportunity to be true to our desires, destiny, nature. This quote might, in fact, say it all (and it was written by a man, go figure):

'That she bear children is not a woman's significance. But that she bear herself, that is her supreme and risky fate.'

D.H LAWRENCE

STORIES OF REGRET AND ACCEPTANCE

Unlike many of the women I have read about or interviewed, I don't question my decision or have regrets about it. I have never romanticised having children, which I think is a big problem in society.

This picture of domestic bliss and happiness, having it all and the knowing smile of fulfilment is constantly shared in media and real life as the holy grail.

This idea is perpetuated that having a baby is the last piece of the puzzle of life, and without the last piece, you are incomplete. Sorry but my life is very complete and happy. It is just different to yours.

I do not regret for one minute the decision I made. I love my life. I love that I can travel, go out, make plans, and have new experiences without burden or restriction. I have a family of my husband and I and our three fur kids. I love what I do. I love my freedom. I love my lifestyle. I love being a crazy rockstar aunty. That is the choice that I made and I am not missing out in any way. I love my life as is.

I know who I am. I am a confident, sassy, effervescent, loyal, kind and smart woman. A fact I am proud of and won't apologise for. I like who I am. I am in love with my life.

When I listen to people whinging about their kids or the fact they have to spend most of their weekend shuttling them to and from activities, I think I dodged a bullet, and it reinforces that I made the right choice for me.

I have been asked too many times to count, 'Won't you regret your decision as you get older?' The answer is no. I can honestly say I have never once 'changed my mind' or 'regretted not having kids' as so many people seem to think I will. I did not regret it at age twenty-five, thirty-five or forty-five, and I will not regret it at sixty-five.

I never think about not having kids when I am old, as we will be travelling, running our own businesses, and exploring. There is a lot I want to achieve and do, and children are not on my bucket list.

And there are many childfree women out there who feel the same way.

Take Lisa, who says, 'I love kids but never wanted my own. I never felt maternal growing up. I wanted to travel and had big career ambitions after uni. People kept telling me that I would change my mind one day, but that never happened. I was in a long-term relationship but we never talked about it. Later I met and married an amazing man. We talked about kids but then found out (with tests) it wouldn't be an option for us. I wasn't particularly upset because I never "got clucky" in the first place.'

Forty-two-year-old Nikki doesn't regret her choices. She has a fatalist perspective and believes fate intervened. 'My journey has not had children in it, so it wasn't meant to be. Who am I to argue with the universe? I don't know whether it's pure biology, with my eggs starting to die off from my mid-thirties, or if it's emotional, or perhaps a combination of both. Most of our friends have children, and we love these families. But we often say how happy we are to be a couple with no kids.

'I still am a big part in the lives of my friends' daughters. I know I will play a big role in those young ladies' lives. They're all either in or approaching their teens now, and I love that I'm that older "Aunty Nik" who they can come to about anything.'

Tracey is also extremely happy to be childfree. 'I am surrounded by beautiful family and friends, some with kids and some without. One thing is that I love children; my decision was never because I did not love children. They are a big part of my life now, thanks to family and friends including me. I often help my friends' children now when they are going through difficult times and they don't want to talk to their parents about it. I feel incredibly blessed. I will never say I made the right decision because I would be lying – I will die not knowing the answer to that. But I made it, I own it, I live with it and I don't second guess it constantly. I get the best of all worlds: I get to play, spoil, give red cordial to and then hand back and wish the parents good luck.'

Leah also doesn't regret her decision not to have a child. 'I have always very been driven and the decisions I make are clear and conscious. I do not regret not having children, but I am also conscious of who I am speaking to as some women can't have children and it's important to be respectful in any occasion discussing this topic. My partner and I have both always felt the same about children and are very happy with just us. We don't feel a child would add or take away from anything we currently have, and we enjoy the benefits of not having children, including regular overseas travel, investing in property and enjoying time with each other.'

Forty-five-year-old Ali Davenport says she knew from a young age she never wanted children. 'As a General Manager of a media business, I have a long-term partner of sixteen years and two dogs that I adore. I'm an aunt of four lovely kids, but I never wanted any of my own. I'm absolutely thrilled that I haven't had kids. Every time I see a screaming child I'm reminded of how lucky I am. Every time I get to go to a restaurant or go away with work without any guilt, I'm reminded of how this couldn't happen so easily with a child. My partner and I are extremely happy not to have children.'

Some women have mixed feelings. Take Jacqui: 'Would I have kids if I had my time over again? No, I wouldn't. But I would most likely have fostered or something along those lines to help kids along as I've always appreciated how horribly difficult and unfair life is for many, many children. But one thing I have realised in stopping to think about these questions is that I truly have loved being a mum, and that the difficulties I have had are mostly due to the beliefs and practices of my husband and therefore how they were raised.'

Lyn, at age fifty-two, says, 'Every now and then I feel the slight sense of regret of not knowing what it would have been like to have kids to admire and enjoy as they grow, but choices are made and I'm happy with that.'

And then there are those who do regret not having children. As an aunt and godmother, fifty-year-old actress Vivica Fox has a beautiful relationship with the children around her. However, she admitted to Oprah that she wishes she had had a child of her own – especially after seeing how happy motherhood made her fellow actresses, like Oscar winner Halle Berry.

'I'll never forget seeing Halle on the red carpet at the Essence [Black Women in Hollywood] Luncheon. She just had her daughter Nahla, and I said, "Wow, she so beautiful." She said, "Vivica, if I knew then what I know now, I would've had five of them... The joy I see in her eyes is just like no other high that I've ever experienced."' It's an experience Fox now says she wishes she could have felt for herself.

Fifty-two-year-old Loretta Ryan never worried about her biological clock until she hit thirty-seven. 'I remember reassuring myself that I'd be fine, I still had time, at least a few more years. My sister-in-law only started her family at forty and she had three kids. I'm fifty-two now, single and still asking the universe why I wasn't given children.

I like to believe there is a reason, that I have another purpose. Yes, I get sad, I cry often when I'm by myself or with my mum.

'The thing that makes me sad is that I don't have a family. I don't have my own children to love and bring up and teach things that my mother and grandmother taught me, memories to make. I have nieces and nephews and I'm bursting with love for them, but it's not the same. I regret not experiencing what it's like to be pregnant and give birth. I've been told when you have a baby, it's an amazing feeling of love for that little being. I regret that I couldn't give my parents grandchildren, even though my two brothers have kids.

'I've watched my girlfriends have children and those children grow up and I feel like I've missed out on a big chunk of life experience that you're meant to have as a woman. In saying all of that, if I'd had kids, my life would be a lot different. I'm sure I would not have achieved the things I've done in my career.'

Then there are women who choose to have children, only to regret it.

One woman I spoke to, who asked to remain anonymous, warns to think hard before becoming a parent. 'I knew raising a child was going to have the difficult and challenging times. But I also expected it to have times of joy and laughter sprinkled with many proud moments. How wrong I was. Sadly, in the fourteen years so far, I can only remember a handful of happy times and one fleeting moment of pride; the rest of the time has been full of anguish, frustrations and disappointment.'

Jae feels ripped off by the experience. 'I look at my kids each and every day and I absolutely love them. I love the people they're becoming. I would give up my life for them. But I would never have changed my mind and had kids if someone, just one person, had been completely honest with me about the costs of having kids and what they have the potential to do to someone like me. Not just the financial burden, but the cost to my own life, my own identity, my own dreams, desires, my own self. It's devastating, and I struggle to deal with it each and every day, especially now as I'm getting older. Everyone is so quick to offer their hearty congratulations when you announce a pregnancy, but no one has the balls to pull you aside and ask, "Are you sure?" or say, "Look, this is what you can expect." No one does that. And I feel ripped off as a result.'

Years ago, I remember a childhood friend saying to me that she was envious of my life. She had married an older man and then had three kids of her own. She envied me being able to travel, go out with friends, get promoted in my job and generally have a carefree lifestyle. I pointed out to her that it was her choice to get married and have three kids. She had chosen her life, just as I had.

Upon reminding her of that, she quickly backtracked and said, 'Of course, I love my kids and my life and I wouldn't change it for the world,' however, I knew she still yearned to have some time to herself.

I also had a number of women comment that they didn't regret their choice, but they never realised how hard motherhood would be. Many were unprepared for what motherhood is really like and wished more women were transparent about what it actually looks like on the other side. Many women I asked said sometimes your body can't do what is expected of you; it is stressful, terrifying, expensive, complicated, messy, selfless and tiring. Given what they know now, many wondered if they would do it all over again.

Not everyone is suited to the mum position, as one Brisbane lady shared with me. 'I am really not suited to the position of mum. I pull it off grandly, but OMFG – I could walk out and never come back half the time. I'm not very maternal. I don't actually regret having children, as I don't do regrets, but it's the hardest thing I've ever lived through. I love them more than life itself but motherhood shouldn't be something entered into lightly and I don't think there is enough education on just how heartbreakingly hard it can be for some.'

When you ask some women whether they would do it again, they openly admit, 'No.' It doesn't mean they love their kids any less; they are merely being honest about doing their time over again. Having been through it, they have said things like, 'Being a parent is not fun,' 'You lose yourself to being a mother,' 'It isn't easy and wonderful,' and 'There are so many other fabulous choices available now.'

Finally, there are many mums who say motherhood is hugely rewarding and nothing compares to the love they have for their children

What these women's stories show is that we are all different. And that is perfectly fine. It doesn't make one woman right and another wrong. We make different choices and rules to suit who we are. We all have our own stories and issues to face; the key is making a decision that won't leave you feeling regret in five, ten, fifteen or twenty years' time.

I, for one, am not satisfied with sitting back and watching life pass me by. I want to dive in the deep end (as long as I don't get my hair wet).

HOW TO MAKE A DECISION YOU DON'T REGRET

Choosing to have children is one of the biggest decisions you will make in your life. One that is irreversible. So, consider it carefully and remember you do have a choice, and it's your right to make your own rules for your life.

The media is awash with warnings about delaying motherhood and the short-sighted selfishness of *career*-hungry women who suddenly realise that motherhood is now or never. The implication is that either these women have been suppressing their maternal drive in pursuit of other rewards and pleasures, or they never had any maternal drive and just want to tick off 'having a baby' from their list.

It's as if there are two kinds of women – the kind that are born wanting a baby and the other kind that might or might not decide to have a baby. Many women find the decision to have a baby agonising because they think they should just know, intuitively, whether they really want one or not. If they don't feel really driven, then maybe they are not cut out for motherhood.

I want this book to help you make considered decisions and to provide practical tips that you can implement to see how the 'mum hat' fits for you.

Here are some ideas to help you with making a decision that will impact your entire life and a few exercises to get you started:

- *Collect field evidence.* Spend time with friends who have kids and watch how it impacts them, how they react, how they interact with other adults, how they look, how they sound, and what they talk about. There is no greater insight into the world of kids than through your friends with kids. Try to spend time with a few different mums, as everyone is different in their approach to parenthood. You want to try and get a holistic view of what it looks like.

- *Spend a day in the life of a mum.* This is a great exercise to fully immerse yourself in motherhood. Spend a full day with a mum of a baby or toddler. And I mean the entire day –from sunrise to sunset. Sleep at their house the night before and do everything they do –wake at same time, follow the routine with them, be with them through feeding, errands, sleeping and every gritty task during the day. If you can, try to spend time with a friend who has a newborn and another one who has a toddler, so you can see the difference. This is a great way to dive into the deep end of the 'mummy pool' before you decide if it's right for you.

- *Babysit for a friend.* Dive right into the deep end and commit to babysitting an infant or toddler and you will get direct insights into what being a mum will be like.

- *Listen to your gut instinct.* The one thing we need to do more as women is listen to our gut instinct. We are intuitive by nature and we instinctively know what is right for us or not. When you think about being a mother, does it feel fulfilling to you?

- *Imagine your future.* Write down how you see your ideal life in five, ten and twenty years' time. Are there children in it? What does it look like? Describe it in detail. Are you going to soccer games and dance recitals or are you travelling and having other adventures? Are you doing both? There is no right or wrong answer, as this is about you and what you want your life to look like in the future.

- *Imagine your life with children.* Sit down in your favourite thinking place – your favourite chair, the beach, wherever you like to sit and think. Now close your eyes and imagine your life with children. How do you feel? Do you feel happy, content and fulfilled? Do you feel overwhelmed, uncomfortable and like you are living in a nightmare? Or does it feel a bit like both?

- *Imagine your life without children.* Follow the same steps as above but this time consider your life without children. How do you feel? Do you feel happy or sad? Does it raise bigger questions for you around your legacy, getting older or regret?

- *Check out some mummy blogs and read the conversations.* This will help give you some insight into the lives of mothers at the coalface and you'll probably read about things your friends might not want to tell you about. We know it is not all sunshine and roses!

- *Be selective about what you read.* It's important to be selective about what you read, however. There are blogs that are pure rants about the joys of having kids, others that treat it like one big nightmare and everything in between. Your goal is to get a balanced view of what it really looks like, not to listen to someone rant and whine. Just Google and you find plenty of commentary around this.

- *Stop playing the 'what if' game.* You cannot keep wondering 'what if?' You have to let go of the fears, the insecurities, the doubt, the scenarios that are playing in your head and accept the decision you make. You cannot spend life looking back in the rear view mirror.

- *Have the talk with the people who are pressuring you.* Explain to them how it makes you feel when they say certain things. You need to be honest with them and try to explain your decision using scenarios they can relate to. It will be a hard conversation, but you will get the chance to share your feelings and get it off your chest. That is healthy for you and for your relationships. They need to know how you feel.

- *Realise it is their issue, not yours, and stop beating yourself up.* Remember you are allowed to make choices and not feel guilty about them. It is your life and not theirs. With acceptance comes release.

TAKE TIME WITH YOUR DECISION

I love this quote from Kathy Lette: 'Children are like Ikea appliances. You have no idea how much assembly is required until it is too late.'

Whether you choose to have children or choose not to, the decision should not be taken lightly. I am not saying that all women make that decision lightly, so please don't jump on me for that comment. However, in this chapter, I've shared stories of women who have said that, if they could have their time again, they would not have children and would've liked a career and to travel.

I don't want that for you.

There are no certainties in life and you can regret having kids just as you can regret not having kids. You can say the same about anything in life. Will you regret taking that new job, getting married, buying a new house, moving to a new city...? In all cases, though, you will be less likely to regret your decision if you put thought into it, and if you make it for the right reasons.

As Tracey says, 'I try not to ever use the word regret. I certainly often think about how my life would have been different, sometimes I even wonder if I made the right decision, but I have always been a person who owns my decisions, so I just get over myself and move my energy into places I do have control over going forward. The baby ship has well and truly sailed out of the harbour.'

'I've thought about this a lot lately. I never thought I'd be this age and not have kids, but my life has also gone in a million ways I never anticipated. I kept feeling like I'd wake up with absolute clarity, and I haven't. And we have a pretty great life together. The chance that we'll regret it doesn't seem like a compelling enough reason to do it. I may wake up tomorrow with that lightning bolt, and I'll have to scramble to make it happen.'

JENNIFER WESTFELDT

IT'S A CHICK'S CHOICE – NEVER APOLOGISE FOR IT!

Most of the writing for this book was done during a stay with my good friends Darlene and Adam in Cairns. Yes, Darls is the one with four kids and I'm the one with zero. One night, they went off camping and I was left with their little dog Coco for company. I sat with a glass of wine and really thought about my choice. As I looked around at all the family photos, kids' drawings, games and children's lives scattered throughout the house, I asked myself: Is this what I really want, and have I been denying myself all these years? Did I secretly want this and was I too afraid to admit it? Was everyone right?

As I contemplated that question, I can honestly say that my answer was no. No, I don't want that. I don't want the responsibility, the mess, the complications, the loss of freedom, the financial burden of another life, and the potential loss of my identity. I am more than happy for my friends if that is their choice (and they know that), but I know it is not for me.

I have love and freedom. I am with someone who loves my smile, the silly things I do, my bad moods (well, maybe not those so much), my determination, my motivation to succeed and my heart. And I love him dearly for that. That's all I need to make my life complete. I know I am loved unconditionally and I don't need some crazy male journalist telling me otherwise! No child can fill that hole for me, because there is no hole.

Admittedly, I am not perfect (even though I keep telling my hubby I am). I, too, am a juggler. I juggle running a business, learning and growing, being a mum to my three beautiful dogs, managing professional commitments, being an aunty, travelling and spending time with loved ones. Somehow, I also make sure I stay sane (wine helps with that part).

Yes, I am told there are many great things about having a child, but I just don't want those things. There are also many great things you can experience without kids and, for me, many of those are just as great (if not better).

That I have made the right decision is something that I get positive reinforcement on regularly. It happened numerous times just while writing this book. While I was in Cairns for two weeks, I took a solo trip to Green Island. Being a tourist destination, the boat and island were filled with families. As I walked about, carefree with my beach bag and towel, I could feel the envious look of one woman in particular. With her husband trying to control two errant toddlers as she pushed the pram and juggled multiple bags, I could feel her struggle. Did I feel like I was missing out? Not a chance in hell. My day was spent on a secluded beach on the island followed by a relaxed lunch of salad and wine. I had a great time and my experience would've been vastly different with children.

I believe women can be more than just mothers. We are business-women, friends, lovers, wives, entrepreneurs, leaders, students, sisters, role models, politicians, CEOs, aunties, executives and board members. We have many titles. 'Mother' might be one of them, but it doesn't have to be.

A very key word in this book is the C word (no, not that one!). The C word I am referring to is 'choice' with a big, fat, capital C.

The notion of a woman expressing choices, previously only available to men, terrifies some people, as it means that women are choosing to live a life for themselves, not for a man or for family obligation. As a whole person, she cannot be defined by the title of 'mother'.

I am passionate about women making their own choices in life. Choices that suit their needs and desires. Why should anyone tell you what you are allowed to do with your body and your life?

And along with making the decision is having that decision support-ed, regardless of which path you choose. Support extends much further than them simply accepting the choice.

Saying you support a woman's choice and showing you do are two different things. I have some friends and family, for example, who never really ask me about my business or what I am doing or what I am working on. While I am expected to have conversations about their children, they barely acknowledge my life choices. This really hurts, especially when they show obvious disinterest in my life and will often just change the subject.

It became even more evident when I set up a crowdfunding cam-paign to get this book published. The lack of support from a number of people I thought were behind me can never be erased and will forever change those relationships. Support goes both ways, and I have *always* supported my friends' and families' decision to have children, including all the gifts that go along with it. To not have that reciprocated speaks volumes to me.

I, along with many other childfree women, hope the stigma surrounding childfree women will eventually fade as society becomes more diverse and accepting of our different choices. We are very lucky to be able to make the decision not to have kids. In fact, we are one of the first generations in the history of the world that, as long as we are careful, can have almost 100 per cent control over our reproductive systems. Think of how many women there are in history who would have chosen not to reproduce if they had a choice, but ended up having ten kids that they did not want or could ill afford.

Childfree women are not looking for your permission to not have a child, but we are looking for your support, acceptance and understanding of our choice as our friend, family or fellow woman.

Ultimately, the choice is yours. And women across the board agree. Here's what some of them had to say:

Ali Davenport: 'I think each to their own. Not having children is a valid choice nowadays. A lot of women I talk to say that they absolutely love their kids, but they could imagine a nice life without them. Now these aren't bad mothers, they are just honest women who have realised what a commitment having a child is. It's full on. It's 24/7 and it goes for at least eighteen years. My view is have kids, or don't have kids, but make sure it's your decision, because it will affect you for the rest of your life.'

MAKING THE RIGHT CHOICE FOR YOU

Tracey: 'If you want to have kids, great, go for it. For those of us who don't want kids, leave us alone and be happy for us. Let everyone make their own choices in life, stop the judgement and be happy for those who just want to get on with life, kids or no kids. We can all have what we want; you just have to be mindful of your choices.'

If you are ambivalent or undecided about parenthood, hopefully this book has shown you the different elements around you that might be subtly influencing your decision, along with giving you some tools to reflect on what is right for you. At the end of the day, this is a choice that only you can make, and you need to make it for yourself. It is not a competition between the mums and non-mums.

So, regardless of whether you are childfree, childless, child friendly or child adjacent (or whatever label you choose), it is about mutual respect and support for our choices as women. Isn't that what sisterhood is about?

Whatever the choices or circumstances of childlessness, the only way to live a meaningful and happy life is to live an authentic life by choosing what is right for you, not living by the measure of what family, society, media or the church believes is the 'right' choice. And the only one who can make that authentic choice is you.

You have one life and only you can decide how to live it. I don't think you should make the choice to have children due to obligation, peer pressure or expectation. I am, and have always been, a believer in choosing what is best for you and making your own rules in life.

Your life is meant to be lived by you and for you. It is up to you to choose your own happily ever after. Blaze your own glittery path and never let anyone dull your sparkle.

SENDING BIG LOVE AND LOTS OF SPARKLE

Special thanks to my fabulous husband Shayne for putting up with me during this process and letting me dig into the now sorry-looking savings account to help bring the book to life. You are the wind beneath my wings (might have borrowed that line from somewhere...) *Xo*

Thank you to Darlene Hallett for letting me crash at your house while I wrote most of this book and always being the fabulous supportive friend you have always been.

Thank you to the amazing people who supported my crowdfunding campaign. Without your support, this book might not have been possible.

Thank you to the women who graciously shared their stories with me. You are all rockstars!

Thank you to the women before me, who inspired me and who have been brave enough to stand up and say, 'I am childfree and I won't accept your judgement anymore.'

And a big thank you to my kickass editor Jacqui and her team at

Grammar Factory for keeping me focused, structured and on deadline and for encouraging me to open my mind further than I had imagined I ever would with this book.

Finally, to my childfree chicks, thank you for playing by your own rules and never letting anyone dull your sparkle.

Thank you

ABOUT THE AUTHOR

Tanya Williams is the effervescent, high energy, driven, sparkly Chief of Everything at Digital Conversations.

By day she wears many fabulous hats – tradigital strategist, outsourced digital manager, digital coach, blogger, digital trainer and speaker. Not to mention being a wife, mother to three fur kids and author of several eBooks, and she does it all while wearing four-inch heels.

By night she is an author and childfree advocate who is passionate about mentoring and helping women learn how to find their inner princess, make their own rules, and make sure they never let anyone dull their sparkle.

Tanya is a big supporter of charities including RSPCA, Kiva and One Girl. Giving back and making a positive impact on people's lives is very important to her.

She is a passionate believer that women should make their own rules in life. No one has the right to force you to do what you don't want to do or to pass judgement on the choices you make.

She wants to be a champion for childfree women and her personal mantra is: Never let anyone dull your sparkle. (Oh, yes, and she loves pink.)

Connect with Tanya
Email: tanya@digitalconversations.com.au
Website: www.digitalconversations.com.au
Twitter & Instagram: Digital_Tanya
LinkedIn and Facebook: Digital Conversations
You Tube: Digital Conversations

Tanya, Tia, Latte & Neo on
her birthday

Tanya & husband Shayne
in New York

Tanya & shoe designer
Jimmy Choo

Tanya at Women in Business
Awards Cocktail event

Our
childfree
lives

Tanya cruising in the Caribbean

Tanya & Shayne,
Brooklyn Bridge New York

Tanya showing off her new Choos

Tanya in one of her favourite
spots - the beach

Lyn & Rohan receiving the RE/MAX
Diamond award

Lyn & Rohan in Paris

Lyn & Rohan Route 66 USA

Nikki & Steve cruising
to Hayman Island

Nikki & Steve at a school in Vietnam

Nikki in Paris

Cate and husband Darrell enjoying
a trip to the snow

Cate and husband Darrell

Cate and husband Darrell
flying high

Michelle and Jeremy in Venice

Michelle in London

Michelle and Jeremy in
Chefchaouen, Morocco

Tracey and her beloved dog Brandi

Tracey & Brandi on their boat

Tracey, husband Rick and Brandi
cruising in their boat

SPREAD THE WORD – SPEAKING OPPORTUNITIES

Tanya is available for speaking opportunities. Her goal is to change social dialogue about being childfree and part of this includes speaking at events and conferences around the globe to ensure this becomes reality.

Her key message is around the C word – choice, and turning judgement into support for all women, regardless of the choices they make in their own lives.

Tanya is a highly engaging, energetic speaker who is passionate about her message and helping other women to make their own rules in life.

Some of the topics Tanya Speaks on:

- Walk a Mile in My Choo's
- Making Your Own Rules
- Living a Childfree Happily Ever After
- Several digital-marketing-centric topics (digital marketing being her business!)

For more information, bookings and bulk book sales enquiries, please email: tanya@digitalconversations.com.au.

"Never let anyone dull your sparkle"

Lightning Source UK Ltd.
Milton Keynes UK
UKHW02f0140080318
319073UK00004B/194/P